PRIMARY PREVENTION OF PSYCHIATRIC DISORDERS

Primary Prevention

THE CLARENCE M. HINCKS

EDITED BY

F. C. R. Chalke M.D.

J. J. Day M.D.

Published for the
Ontario Mental Health Foundation
by University of Toronto Press

# of Psychiatric Disorders

MEMORIAL LECTURES, 1967

BY *C. A. Roberts* M.D.

Including
MEDICAL ASPECTS OF PRIMARY PREVENTION
OF PSYCHIATRIC DISORDERS,
papers presented at the University of Ottawa,
February 1967, by
W. HARDING LE RICHE

MORTON BEISER

R. C. A. HUNTER

JOHN A. RASSELL

BENJAMIN GOLDBERG

V. A. KRAL

A. LAMBERTI

D. G. MCKERRACHER

J. D. GRIFFIN

V. SZYRYNSKI

Contents

Foreword

When, in 1965, the Ontario Mental Health Foundation established an annual lectureship to stimulate professional workers in the field of mental health, it seemed only natural that the lectures should be named in honour of the late Clarence Meredith Hincks, a pioneer in the development of mental-health therapy and the founder of the Canadian Mental Health Association.

It was the aim of the Foundation to make it possible for those engaged in training and research in psychiatric and related disciplines to hear, and more particularly to associate on a professional footing with, persons of outstanding stature in their chosen fields. In furtherance of this purpose the locale of the lectures was not to be fixed but was to move among the faculties of medicine of the universities of Ontario.

The University of Ottawa graciously accepted the invitation of the Foundation to sponsor the inaugural series of lectures and selected as the lecturer Dr. Charles A. Roberts, the Executive Director of the Clarke Institute of Psychiatry, Toronto. His lectures were delivered in Ottawa on February 2, 3, and 4, 1967. It will always be a source of satisfaction to the Foundation that Mrs. Hincks was in the audience on the occasion of the first lecture.

While making no firm commitment as to publication, the Foundation expected, as has been borne out by Dr. Roberts' lectures, that material written for presentation under the ægis of the lectureship would, of itself, merit publication. Accordingly, the Foundation is pleased to present this volume embodying the first Clarence M. Hincks Memorial Lectures, to which have been added papers presented during the same conference by experts on various medical aspects of the prevention of psychiatric disorders.

While the choice of subject for the lectures is that of the lecturer, it is gratifying that the emphasis in the first lectures should have been upon the mental health needs of the community and the manner in which they can be met. Without in any way deprecating the role of pure research, to the support of which the Foundation has contributed extensively, the subject of these lectures serves to emphasize another area of interest of the Foundation, and its awareness of its responsibility to seek to improve the quality and extent of mental health services in the Province of Ontario.

ARTHUR KELLY
The Ontario Mental Health Foundation

Clarence Meredith Hincks, B.A., M.D., D.SC., LL.D.
1885-1964

"We must become concerned with the mental health needs of every man, woman and child in the community, because the truth is being borne upon us that everybody is confronted with mental problems of one kind or another. . . . We will never be able to solve the problem of mental illness until we can stop it at its source. We must learn how to prevent it from developing in the first place." These words are typical of those used by the late Clarence Meredith Hincks on many occasions in both public addresses and private discussions. The idea became almost an obsession with him.

The concept of a preventive programme was probably first discussed with Dr. C. K. Clarke during one of the sessions of the out-patient clinic for mental disorders which was organized in 1914 at the Toronto General Hospital. Clarke had invited Dr. Hincks and Dr. O. C. J. Withrow to join him in this enterprise. The clinic had become very well known and tremendously active. Hincks was finally disenchanted with the effect of the diagnostic and treatment procedures then available. "All we do" he said, "is to lend a sympathetic ear and try to understand what went wrong. Occasionally we have to commit a patient to the mental hospital. And the crowds of patients coming for help get bigger all the time." The search for a solution to this problem led Hincks, with Clarke's blessing, to New York and to Clifford Beers. In 1918, with Beers' help and Clarke's professional backing, he started the Canadian National Committee for Mental Hygiene (now the Canadian Mental Health Association). But the name of Hincks is also associated with a great many progressive developments in the mental-health field ranging all the way from better facilities and programmes for the mentally retarded to the introduction of modern and humane treatment programmes for the mentally ill. He was the moving spirit, initiator, and promoter of new developments and services important to psychiatry and for more than half a century he dedicated himself to forging a working partnership between psychiatry, the social sciences, and the lay public.

Born in St. Mary's, Ontario, in 1885, he acquired from his parents both a sensitivity concerning people in trouble and the habit of service. His mother was a teacher and his father was a dedicated and successful Methodist clergyman. Hincks graduated from medical school at the University of Toronto in 1907 and began general practice in Campbell-ford and then in Toronto. While his practice was developing, he restlessly pursued a number of part-time activities which included the post of medical officer in the Toronto schools. Here he became convinced that many of the children who were referred to him were suffering from mental problems rather than physical disorders. This aroused his interest in mental hygiene and he began to widen the range of his activities in this field. In 1913 he became a consultant to the newly organized Juvenile Court in Toronto and came to the attention of Dr. C. K. Clarke who was then Professor of Psychiatry, Dean of Medicine, and Superintendent of the Toronto General Hospital.

Hincks was the first secretary of the Canadian National Committee for Mental Hygiene. Dr. Clarke was the first Medical Director and on his death in 1924 Hincks became the Medical and then General Director – a post which he held for nearly 30 years. The Committee had as a top priority the establishment of a preventive programme: it also undertook a wide range of activities of which the most dramatic were the surveys of mental hospitals and institutions throughout Canada. Hincks and his colleagues, finding that conditions in most of these were appalling, were able to persuade governments in all provinces to undertake needed reforms. In addition, Hincks began mental-hygiene surveys of school children, encouraging the use of intelligence tests and the organization of special classes for the retarded.

During the early twenties, Dr. Hincks worked hard to get the long delayed psychiatric "reception" hospital completed in Toronto. Clarke had recommended such an institution some years before. Hincks finally brought the university, the city, and the provincial government together and work began. Clarke was present at the laying of the cornerstone in 1924 but died before the building opened. Hincks suggested that the building be named the Clarke Memorial Institute. While his suggestion was not acted on then, the new psychiatric hospital just recently com-pleted to replace the Toronto Psychiatric Hospital is called the Clarke Institute of Psychiatry. Hincks also helped to organize the Institute of Child Study established in 1925 at the University of Toronto and was able to obtain Rockefeller Foundation assistance to finance it. In the same way, he helped establish a mental-hygiene institute at McGill University in Montreal.

In 1930, Hincks was invited to become Medical Director of the National Committee in New York (now the National Association for Mental Health). He accepted this post on condition that he retain his base and post in Canada. He then began eight years of almost weekly commuting between Toronto and New York. Clifford Beers continued as Secretary. The two men were sufficiently alike in temperament that occasional clashes of personality were inevitable. Both were prone to periodic spells of depression alternating with periods of tremendous energy and optimism.

During the next few years, in spite of a major economic depression, Hincks was able not only to keep the two national committees (Canada and the United States) alive but also was largely responsible for several really outstanding achievements. These included the organization in 1935 of the Schizophrenia Research Programme which was supported by the Scottish Rite Masons, Northern Jurisdiction, and the organization in 1930 of the Committee on Psychiatric Education. He persuaded the Commonwealth Fund to finance an intensive study of psychiatric teaching programmes in the medical schools of the United States and Canada. This led to improvements in the undergraduate and graduate training in this field. He also organized the American Board of Neurology and Psychiatry in 1934. With his prompting, the Commonwealth Fund also supported this project which was developed in the offices of the National Committee and which has done so much to raise the standard of excellence in these two specialties.

Hincks was one of the founders of the International Committee for Mental Hygiene which sponsored two international congresses in 1930 and 1937. Immediately after World War II, he was one of a small group which helped to reconstitute the international organization, and in London, England, in 1948, the World Federation for Mental Health was organized. He served as the Chairman of the Fifth International Mental Health Congress held in Toronto in 1954.

During World War II, Hincks and his Toronto colleagues helped to establish modern psychological and psychiatric services in the Canadian Army. Later, he organized a project by which a corps of uniformed nursery-school workers, teachers, and social workers went overseas to help provide day-nurseries for thousands of children evacuated from the blitzed areas in England.

At the end of the war, Hincks organized a mental-hygiene consultation service to assist the social and welfare agencies in Toronto which had been virtually without psychiatric help for several years. This service finally became the Toronto Mental Health Clinic which will shortly become Canada's first comprehensive, community psychiatric service for children.

Doctor Hincks never claimed to be a great scientist or clinician. He felt he had only one significant talent – infectious enthusiasm for his chosen field. He always gave credit to others and loyally supported his friends, even when they were in error. Although he was a most modest man, he received many honours during his life. These included honorary degrees from the universities of Toronto and British Columbia, life fellowships in the American Psychiatric Association and the American Orthopsychiatric Association, and an honorary life membership in the Canadian Psychiatric Association. He received the first Mental Health Award of the Mental Hygiene Institute of Montreal and the Coronation Medal in 1953. He was a member of the Comité d'honneur of the World Federation for Mental Health.

Doctor Hincks' first wife, Mabel Millman Hincks, died in 1951. He is survived by their three children, Margaret of Toronto, the Rev. Norman William Hincks of Zambia, Africa, and Barbara (Mrs. Jack Toivenan) of Northern Ontario. In 1957, he married Marjorie Keyes who for over 30 years was his secretary and dedicated co-worker.

Mental and emotional illness was familiar to Doctor Hincks in a personal way. Ever since his days as a medical student, he had suffered repeated spells of anxiety, depression, and apathy. Far from feeling discouraged by this disability, he felt it was an asset, for it enabled him to know and understand at first hand some of the suffering of those he was striving so hard to help. In an interview on the national radio network, he freely acknowledged and described his illness. He felt strongly that only by such open admission and the evidence that illness did not impose permanent disability could he change some of the existing public prejudice in connection with mental illness. While these depressed periods did not seem to reduce his accomplishments, they certainly resulted in an unusual pattern of work. When he was feeling well, he accomplished prodigious amounts of work involving travel, conferences, meetings, and fund raising. When he was depressed, he disappeared – usually to his beloved Muskoka Lakes – where he always seemed to be able to recover his health and vigour. He called it "recharging his batteries."

A public crusader in the interests of the mentally ill requires more than sensitivity, compassion, and empathy all of which are helpful but not enough by themselves. Hincks had all these qualities and, in addition, courage, conviction, aggressiveness, and an indignant impatience which kept him going, often in the face of professional and political resentment. He absorbed the hostility of those he criticized without himself becoming hostile. His aggressive indignation was never directed personally but was reserved for the larger issues – obsolete government policies, professional irresponsibility, and public complacency. His greatest enemy was "man's inhumanity to man."

Preface

Primary prevention of psychiatric illnesses is a frequent subject of discussion within the discrete areas of preventive medicine and psychiatry, but at the present time often seems to be dismissed as "peripheral," impractical, or insoluble. In spite of occasional joint conferences devoted to this aspect of medicine there appears to be little cross-fertilization of ideas, agreement on objectives, or mutual endeavour. It may be that we should determine the reasons for this neglect by examining some of the current issues.

In using the expression "primary" prevention we are combining the first two categories in the now widely accepted classification of Leavell of Harvard: (a) general health promotion, and (b) specific protection (early diagnosis and limitation of disability being the secondary level with rehabilitation being the tertiary level). Because mental ill-health in any one individual has social impacts on others, usually to the detriment of all who are touched by the effects of illness, there are, of course, primary preventive aspects to early diagnosis and limitation of disability. This point is stressed both in the second Hincks Lecture and in the papers by McKerracher on the "Role of the General Practitioner" and Szyrynski on "Crisis Care" as factors in primary prevention.

The classical paradigm of primary preventive action when the specific pathogenic agent is still undiscovered, the removal of the Broad Street pump handle by Dr. John Snow a century ago in London, is well known to all physicians. Most of us seem to picture this figure, following a sudden flash of intuitive knowledge, rushing to destroy, singlehandedly, the offending pump. At the conference on prevention and community mental health held in St. Louis in 1964, Hassler described the historical situation more precisely. What actually happened was that, after years of study utilizing the epidemiological evidence of the day, Snow had arrived at the rational hypothesis that sewage contamination of the water supply bore a possible relationship to the incidence of cholera.

Wishing to test this hypothesis he persuaded the constitutionally appointed local authorities to co-operate with his project, and to permit the removal of the pump handle on a trial basis.

Today, specific pathogenic factors in the etiology of mental disorders are no more than hypotheses. To test these it is often necessary to develop effective communication between research scientists, practicing professionals, and the final legislative authority. To improve this communication it is first necessary to examine some of the questions and problems in all the areas, from the scientific to the political, which impede understanding and inhibit action.

On the scientific side these include: (*a*) the need to identify, if possible, those specific measures the alteration of which will remove or reduce necessary or sufficient causes of specific disorders; (*b*) the need to define more adequately these same specific disorders in relation to cause or causes; (*c*) the need to devise means of identifying, measuring, recording, classifying, counting, reassessing, following up, and comparing various groups in the population to determine the impact of one or many putative preventive interventions.

On what one might call the professional-organizational side, other difficulties arise.

(*a*) There is no clear mandate to any specific group, specialty, or administrative facility within medicine to concern itself with the study or implementation of primary preventive measures for mental disorders.

(*b*) There is confusion as to what kinds or degrees of disorders are the responsibility of the medical profession in terms of diagnosis, care, and prevention.

(*c*) Preventive Medicine as a specialty is moving from impersonal, social manipulation of the environment to reduce or remove pathogenic sources of disease, towards individual "clinical" procedures aimed at reducing effects of pathogens of identifiable high-risk groups. The overlap and "cut-off points" between this approach and the role of clinical psychiatry as another specialty are, at present, blurred and fluctuant.

(*d*) The "mental-health clinic" engaged and operated by provincial health departments with general tax funds often devoted part of its efforts to some aspects of primary prevention including public education, consultation of social agencies, and school programmes. The volume and kind of these services were variable and usually uncoordinated and even unknown to local public health authorities; but they did exist. With the trend to have hospital care and medical care costs for psychiatric illness supported on the same basis as for other illnesses, there is less and less opportunity for individuals, and facilities, to devote themselves to this purpose. Thus a hiatus is developing with nobody apparently rushing in to fill it.

Finally, many of the steps that the medical profession can identify, as preventive, can only be applied with the assistance of society at large through legislation, voluntary societies, and public support. The situation is analogous to the prevention of malnutrition or starvation, the greatest public-health problem in the world today. Physicians can advise on the exact amounts of each nutritional requirement, but the social, political, and economic arrangements to make the food available are beyond the capabilities of the medical or any other single profession to bring about. In regard to prevention of psychiatric disorders these other arrangements include: (*a*) the recognition by governments at all levels of the role of each level, consistent with the constitution of a country, in supporting programmes of primary prevention; (*b*) the determination of priorities to be assigned to efforts and expenditures for technical education, physical fitness, entertainment, criminal reformation, housing, standard of income, and prevention of illness; (*c*) the distinctions and conflicts, if any, between the goals and means to enhance mental health and to provide and develop human growth and fulfillment in its broadest sense.

When the opportunity presented itself to the University of Ottawa to sponsor the first Hincks Memorial Lectures in 1967, it seemed a timely occasion to focus on this topic in the presence of interested members of both specialties. Dr. Charles Roberts was invited to deliver these lectures, the main substance of this volume as they were of the postgraduate conference of the Faculty of Medicine on "Primary Prevention of Psychiatric Disorders," held on February 2–4, 1967.

During this conference, attended by both psychiatrists and public-health physicians from federal, provincial, and municipal governments, and universities, a number of authorities presented papers summarizing knowledge and experience and forming the basis of general discussion among those in attendance. Since many of these papers represent a comprehensive coverage of little-known aspects of psychiatry, it seemed appropriate to publish them and thus make available to a wider audience their contents. We consider that the objectives of the conference were achieved in a form of mid-century stocktaking of the state of knowledge and speculation, of what demands further investigation, and of what some of the steps towards application of our knowledge may be. We hope that the articles in the following pages will stimulate this kind of stocktaking among those who were not present at the conference itself.

J. J. D.
F. C. R. C.

PART ONE

Clarence M. Hincks Memorial Lectures 1967

DR. C. A. ROBERTS

DR. CHARLES A. ROBERTS
Hincks Memorial Lecturer, 1967

Dr. Charles Roberts was chosen by the University of Ottawa to be the first Clarence M. Hincks Memorial Lecturer. As an associate professor of psychiatry and preventive medicine at the University of Toronto he combines both of the medical specialties most intimately concerned with the prevention of psychiatric disorders. He brings to the task a long and varied experience in administrative psychiatry which qualifies him to consider not only the scientific aspects but, in addition, the constitutional, organizational, and practical problems of implementation in this country and its provinces.

Born in Newfoundland, he received his early education there, later graduating in medicine from Dalhousie University. Following a period of military service during World War II he became the superintendent, in succession, of the St. John's Hospital for Nervous and Mental Diseases, and of the St. John's General Hospital in Newfoundland. Next he was appointed chief of the Mental Health Division of the Department of National Health and Welfare, a post he filled with distinction, and with his appointment as secretary of the Canadian Psychiatric Association became not only well known from coast to coast in Canada but well aware of the problems of each province. In 1957 he became executive director of the Douglas Hospital in Verdun, Quebec, which position he retained until 1965 when he moved to a similar post at the Clarke Institute of Psychiatry at the University of Toronto.

His interests and associations range widely including positions as an examiner in hospital administration and as a member of public health associations and of expert committees of the World Health Organization. The breadth of his interests makes it possible for him to see the many facets of medical and social problems from a range of viewpoints.

As one of the authors of *More for the Mind*, the blueprint for the growth of psychiatric services in Canada, as a president of the Canadian Psychiatric Association, as the chairman of the National Scientific Council of the Canadian Mental Health Association, he has been not only a student of, but also a powerful influence on, the development of psychiatry in Canada.

Introduction

To be selected as the first Hincks Memorial Lecturer is an honour of which I am very conscious. I first met Dr. Hincks during the second world war when I was in Toronto for further training in psychiatry. He was involved with, and excited and enthusiastic about the arrangements made to help with evacuated children in Great Britain and Canada and was enthusiastically looking forward to the further development of psychiatry in the post-war years. When I was appointed superintendent of the Hospital for Mental and Nervous Diseases in St. John's, Newfoundland, immediately after the termination of hostilities, I was keenly aware of my need for help, guidance, and support. I naturally thought of Dr. Hincks and arranged for him, as a representative of the then National Committee on Mental Hygiene, to carry out a survey for us. I well remember the three weeks he and Marjorie Keyes spent in Newfoundland. As a result of his report – perhaps more of his meetings with the Commissioner of Health and the Governor – we were able to initiate rapid and meaningful improvements in the development of psychiatric services in Newfoundland. I realized then, and I have become more acutely aware since, that the advocacy of improved psychiatric services is not a popular cause. I doubt very much that it ever can be so long as there is such a remarkable absence of community participation in the organization, administration, and development of psychiatric services. Vested interests have certain well-recognized characteristics: they are self-protective, they resent unfavourable criticism, and, while being remarkably effective in terms of self-preservation, they are equally resistant to change, even from within. I am sure that Dr. Hincks was never popular with vested-interest groups; I hope he was respected for his unfailing devotion to the cause of the mentally ill and his never failing optimism with respect to the promotion of mental health.

I have always been conscious of the impact on my career and my attitudes of my wartime experiences in the services. I try to govern many of my activities on the basis of instruction received in the army before I became a training officer at Camp Borden. Of the essence of this training to prepare us as officers and instructors was the principle that it is easy to gain popularity and equally easy to lose it, but devotion to a cause and to one's fellow men, frankness, and honesty, will, in the long run, lead to a more lasting respect which will stand in good stead in times of stress. I think Dr. Hincks was respected for his efforts in the field of mental health. He certainly was one of those who have had a terrific impact on me. I have twice left the mental-health field only to return because I know of no other area of human service which can give so much satisfaction – and so much frustration – and where, in spite of frequent public misinterpretation of our motives, it is possible to recognize ever-increasing community support for our efforts. These lectures on primary prevention, inadequate as they may be, constitute my tribute to the leadership given by Dr. Hincks and recognize his hope – and the hope of all of us – that we will someday find more specific ways to promote better mental health and prevent more mental illnesses.

Acknowledgment is gratefully given to a number of individuals who, by their contacts with me, have affected this presentation: Dr. R. O. Jones, my professor of Psychiatry at medical school and a life-long friend, Dr. Paul Lemkau, Dr. J. D. M. Griffin, Dr. D. G. McKerracher, Dr. A. B. Stokes, and many other colleagues too numerous to mention. I have received specific help from Dr. D. B. Coates of the Clarke Institute, Miss M. J. Bolduc, a master's student at the School of Hygiene, and my secretaries, Mrs. E. Hall and Mrs. G. Scrase, who have faithfully typed and prepared these manuscripts.

C.A.R.

1   Primary Prevention: To the Present

As I prepared these lectures, I became increasingly aware of a considerable amount of relevant literature: so extensive that I could only conclude that we really don't know too much about primary prevention in the field of mental health. I am sure you would agree that the more specific our knowledge and its application, the more likely it is that we will find concise, specific literature which readily communicates present and accumulated knowledge to us. I am including with these discussions a bibliography – by no means complete – but sufficient to indicate the extent of the literature and to give some reasonable references for a more detailed study of this topic.

Seminars, institutes, conferences, conventions, and committee meetings are becoming more and more a part of our way of life. I cannot help but question the impact of such meetings on the health resources and manpower available to the population of our country. The size of our problem, the shortage of personnel, the absence of adequate facilities, and our inadequate knowledge of morbidity and cause could easily immobilize us. On the other hand, we must find ways and means not only to expand our resources but to utilize those we have to maximum advantage. I am sure that interpersonal and group activities are essential in the field of mental health and I often wonder if we could not make more professional time available to people in our communities for such activities even at the expense of some of the many professional meetings, seminars, and so on which we are continually under pressure to attend. I was very impressed by a recent statement by Dr. Harvey Tompkins, president of the American Psychiatric Association, who, while recognizing the inadequacies of psychiatric knowledge, stated that the full application of our present knowledge in the clinical field, empirical as it may be, could dramatically change the present morbidity and mental health of people in our many communities suffering from psychiatric illnesses.

In many discussions one hears the terms "mental health," "mental illness," and "psychiatry" used almost interchangeably. This practice reached a remarkable level when a misprint (or was it a misprint?) occurred in the report of the Joint Commission on Mental Health and Mental Illness in the United States: "Mental Health is our number one problem and we must stamp out mental health." Surely it is mental illness which is one of our major health problems and which we wish to stamp out!

In other fields of medicine, there seem to be much less confusion between primary prevention and treatment; the cardiologist deals with treatment comprehensively and when preventive measures, such as the use of penicillin in rheumatic illnesses, of wide or universal application are available he assists public-health personnel, health educators, and other community services to apply these preventive measures to the population at risk. One wonders if those to whom we act as consultants, and even we ourselves, would not be less confused if these two aspects were clearly defined. The promotion of mental health and the prevention of psychiatric illnesses are surely causes to which we are all devoted and to which we must allocate a considerable part of our efforts but there are present in our society many endemic mental illnesses for which we do not at this time have primary preventive measures available. We may, amongst ourselves, recognize primary, secondary, and tertiary activities but many of our professional colleagues and most people in our communities think of primary activities alone as being preventive.

Psychiatry is the medical specialty concerned with diseases of the mind; psychiatrists are medical specialists concerned with these diseases. As the main objective of all medicine is the elimination of illness, so the main objective of psychiatry is the prevention of psychiatric illness. On the other hand mental health should more appropriately be seen as a broader field which concerns itself with the whole range of psycho-social problems and the promotion of more effective living. While many may not agree with me, I believe that people in many disciplines are qualified to participate in and direct mental-health programmes; it is not an exclusive prerogative of psychiatry nor are psychiatrists necessarily the best qualified to direct such programmes. Equally, however, I believe that a sick person is morally and legally a medical responsibility and thus I must believe that patients with psychiatric illness should be examined and treated by physicians. Many other disciplines will participate in their treatment but responsibility for the treatment rests with the physician. In a recent paper (1) Paul Lemkau says ". . . the term 'mental illness' is a misnomer . . . the term could hide some important issues in thinking about the prevention of mental illnesses. In my estimation, it has done so. It leads one to think of a prevention and treatment programme that would prevent and treat all kinds of mental illnesses. It seeks to apply a panacea rather than to deal with the multiple, specific and treatment needs. . . ."

Efforts to define mental health have been notoriously unsuccessful. It is my belief that our efforts to obtain an understanding or appreciation of mental health should be directed towards the reality in which we live and not to abstract conceptual models of what constitutes mental health.

It may appear that I am reviewing certain aspects of our way of life which are well known to all of us, but few of us think about these matters; a consideration of them seems desirable to set the stage for the discussion which follows. The average community has developed a set of mores on the basis of which individuals are expected to follow certain patterns of behaviour. If we follow a pattern we are acceptable to the community around us but are rejected if we deviate too far. We must also bear in mind that communities in the western world have two ways of expressing severe rejection. One is admitted to a hospital if considered to be ill; alternatively, one comes under the judicial, penal, or reform system if considered able, but unwilling, to conform to the mores of our society.

The average member of our communities is expected to involve him or herself, during each twenty-four-hour period, in a constructive and productive activity – work – averaging about eight hours per day; to participate in recreational or similar pursuits for about the same period of time; and to have a period of rest which, for the average person, is also about eight hours. It is important for the present discussion that we ask ourselves why people follow this pattern. It is easy but too superficial to suggest that we do it just because we grew up in this particular culture. Certainly most of us have never given this matter any thought and we follow the routine almost like zombies even though we frequently have a terrific resentment against the demands made upon us.

The average person rests six, seven, or eight hours per night because by the late teens or early twenties he has learned from experience the routine he must follow in order to function reasonably well. We all know that we can go one or possibly two or even three nights without having our regular amount of rest, but we know equally well that to do more than this is to endanger our health and to render us inefficient for a short period of time until we regain our equilibrium. There appear to be three main objectives of those who work: that satisfaction that comes from doing something ourselves, recognition of the value of our activities by society, and the obtaining of a livelihood. The role of recreation appears to be to supply a change of activity and an opportunity to do something for pleasure rather than for income. There is good reason to believe that there is only one real difference of motivation insofar as work and recreation are concerned: we work in order to gain a living whereas in recreation we can make a choice of activity purely on the basis of inclination. We can do something which gives us personal satisfaction, which has sufficient recognition from our own family, our own friends, and social contacts but without having to be concerned about its value in terms of dollars and cents.

I would, if time were available, give much more consideration to this discussion as I believe this whole area is of the utmost importance in the prevention of mental illnesses and the treatment of patients. I would suggest that the acceptance of the above routine together with a positive identification of the individual with one or more of the people with whom he has continuing contact or who is responsible for his therapy are the most important factors in the treatment and prevention of all forms of disability.

People in our society appear to be ever more confused about their objectives and to be increasingly involved in a search for satisfying activities as the status of and respect for work in our society changes. I must express a great deal of personal concern about the attitudes of therapists and other gate-keepers with regard to work. I am satisfied that many of our present social and professional difficulties are due to an over-emphasis on making a living with the shortest possible work week and that too little emphasis is given to personal satisfaction and to social recognition of the part the individual plays in our society.

Traditionally, our communities have placed a high value on work and participation; those who can afford to not work are frequently referred to as playboys and spendthrifts. Historically, the only people excused from work are the sick or dependent; all others who do not work are considered lazy or in some other way undesirable. The group of dependent people includes the very young and the very old who, either because of lack of development or because of progressive aging, are unable to participate in work. The introduction of various welfare programmes and, more particularly, unemployment insurance has further complicated this matter. In general, unemployment insurance funds as presently administered are misnamed for they are used to guarantee income and not employment. A guarantee of income is quite different from a guarantee of employment. Socially, it would be much more appropriate to ensure that work would be available for everyone than to be concerned with income maintenance: the guarantee of work would ensure income maintenance, whereas the guarantee of income alone may well interfere with the normal motivations of our society. It is even suggested that there are now a good many people who will work for a certain length of time in order to qualify for unemployment insurance and then will not work again until their benefits have been used up.

Now comes a most important question. What does all of this mean to the average person in our community and to the psychiatric patient? What does it mean to professionals? It is important to maintain a reasonable perspective with regard to these matters. Formerly, it was necessary to work long hours because modern means of production were not available to us. As our means of production have improved, it has become possible to shorten work hours for the needs of our communities can be met more quickly. It should be noted here that reference is made to production and not to personal-care services. While technology has made surplus production possible, it has not had the same effect on the service industries. In education, health, welfare, and related personal-care services the shortened work week and changes in attitude towards work have only increased our problem – we are probably further away from meeting the needs of our population and the situation seems to be deteriorating. Increased emphasis on formal education, longer holidays, shorter hours, and so on seem to increase our basic shortage of personnel faster than we can increase the numbers available; one wonders if we can ever meet the needs of our population while the present trends continue.

The shortened hours of work have accentuated the importance of recreation. Furthermore, it is quite obvious that most workers engaged in mass production are unable to meet the needs of personal satisfaction and social recognition; their dissatisfaction is continuously expressed by demands for more and more income with less and less work. People do not talk about the lack of personal satisfaction or status of the service which they perform as this requires the admission of a personal problem, or leads to a criticism, explicit or implicit, of one's superiors or the organization in which one is employed; facing a problem in this way is unacceptable to most people. It is in this area that I believe professional people are most confused. Professionals, as part of the communities in which they live, want a shortened work week, higher salaries, and other fringe benefits obtained by labour. At the same time they wish to obtain personal satisfaction and social recognition for the services they perform. It is quite possible that these two objectives are incompatible.

At this time, reference must be made to a paper by Dr. Bernard L.

Bloom, of the Department of Psychology, University of Colorado (2).
In discussing the appropriateness of the medical or biological model as
against the miasma theory in the field of mental health, he quotes
Shryock (3) as follows: "The conviction that the quickest way to
improve the health of the poor was through sanitation received statistical
validation during the 1850's when various British towns showed marked
mortality declines following the establishment of sanitary controls. . . .
At the same time that sanitation promised so much, direct medical care
of the poor seemed to promise little. . . . It is no wonder that lay
reformers . . . had more confidence in what mathematics could do for
the poor than they had in medicine."

Bloom states:

The model introduced by the practices of the miasmatists should be carefully
considered by professionals entering the field of community mental health.
Its successes were outstanding, albeit for the wrong reasons. As was
previously noted, the field of public health was begun by miasmatists. While
the practice of community mental health involves interaction with programmes in welfare, in education, as well as in general health, it represents,
in part, the application of basic public health concepts to the mental disorders. These concepts, introduced so usefully more than a century ago,
include: (1) an emphasis upon primary prevention rather than on treatment
or rehabilitation; (2) an emphasis on the total community rather than on
the individual; and (3) the recognition that progress is made by working
with and through community agencies, that is, that communities are
organized and that this community organization is a powerful and relevant
force in the service of improving a community's emotional well-being.

In a sense, miasma theory suffered from being insufficiently precise.
Imbedded within its borders was a small but important island of validity.
Until the reasons for their effectiveness were properly understood, miasmatists were concerned about much which, in retrospect, was not within their
proper scope of interest. This phenomenon has probably characterized many
other theories as well. Certainly the contemporary community mental health
professional is being attacked for his involvement in areas such as poverty,
urban renewal, and social disequilibrium, which people consider outside the
direct scope of mental health. Yet, as one examines the current state of
knowledge in the field and the array of hypotheses available to anyone particularly interested in the prevention of emotional disorders, the miasma model
seems entirely appropriate. It may be that the theories which lie behind the
practice of community mental health—and this paper has sought to show how
similar these theories actually are to those of the miasmatists—may one day
also be considered naive. But in return for results equivalent to those
obtained by the sanitarians and engineers in the prevention of infectious
diseases, we might willingly pay the price.

Primary prevention, in its strictest sense, covers those measures and
activities which will reduce the number of cases of a disorder or illness

in the community. Or, in other words, "Prevention may be accomplished in the pathogenesis period by measures designed to promote general optimum health or by specific protection of a man against disease agents or the establishment of barriers against agents in the environment." (4) The goal of secondary prevention is to lower the frequency of sick persons in the community through the successful treatment of established cases and, particularly, through early treatment of such disorders so that the total number of cases of the disorder is reduced and the acute and chronic phases of the illness are prevented from developing. The concept of tertiary prevention includes all of those measures, other than or in addition to the treatment of the disease, which are designed to reduce the frequency and severity of the disability associated with mental illness. That much of the disability seen in the mentally ill is not necessarily inherent to the disease-process is a basic assumption. Social crippling is often a by-product of the social experiences and deprivations to which the mentally ill are commonly subjected. (5)

At the present time, we do not know the specific cause of many mental disorders. We do, however, have some useful assumptions about what may encourage or discourage the development of mental health. In the field of nutrition, for example, we are familiar with the importance of supplying the body with the right food, vitamins, calories, etc., to meet changing physical needs and to protect and enhance normal growth and development. In mental health, there are psychic, social, and physical needs which must be satisfied if mental health is to be protected and promoted. Knowledge of these psychological "vitamins" is increasing. We have known for generations that love, tenderness, and affection are essential for the healthy emotional growth of an infant and child. Adults, including the aged, have emotional needs which must be met if good mental health is to be maintained and psychiatric illness avoided.

As in other fields of health, the child is of primary importance in preventive activities. Parents, teachers, the clergy, recreational workers, and others associated with the child as it develops must be similarly concerned about psychological development and must be informed about the emotional, social, psychological, and physical needs of the young. They must know how to provide adequate opportunities for healthy emotional development and must anticipate the critical reactions which can occur when too much stress is combined with inadequate satisfaction of emotional needs. "Community Psychiatry" and "Social Psychiatry" are typical of the names which have been applied to such a community responsibility approach to mental-health programmes.

While we know that psychiatric illnesses and symptoms are extremely common, the true extent of morbidity in this field is difficult to establish and is very largely dependent on the definitions used in any particular study. It is variously estimated that 1 in 10 of the non-institutionalized population has some recognizable psychiatric illness or defect but some studies report that nearly half the population show some signs of psychiatric disorder or precursor symptoms. According to Kraft (6): "The recently issued volumes of the Joint Commission on Mental Illness and Health present us with a wealth of documentation establishing the proliferating roots of mental ill health and its connection with a multitude of related social problems, such as delinquency, poverty, and alcoholism. A recent study of mental health in Manhattan concludes that as many as one out of four adults has levels of mental ill health requiring treatment." It is more than possible that no other illnesses afflict our population to such an extent regardless of how we estimate the incidence of psychiatric illnesses. It is considered, though, that some common types of psychiatric illnesses may be as much diseases of our society as they are diseases of individuals in our society.

While a number of psychiatric illnesses have recognized causes such as brain damage, infections, poisoning, injury, dietary deficiencies, and physical illness, these illnesses account for only a small part of the psychiatric illness seen in our society. Some illnesses, especially in the field of mental deficiency, seem to be family-related and may be either acquired or inherited or both. It is clear, however, that we do not know whether most psychiatric illnesses have physical causes, or are inherited, according to specific genetic patterns, that in fact, we do not yet know their specific causes.

Prevention must be attempted, as it is increasingly obvious that treatment alone can never deal with such widespread illnesses. Our country cannot provide enough trained personnel to ensure that all patients with psychiatric symptoms and illnesses receive adequate treatment. These preventive programmes must be developed even in the face of our ignorance of specific causes and of the natural course of many psychiatric conditions.

We must also face up to the fact that many of the services provided in our society to deal with social breakdown and psychiatric illness may, in fact, worsen or prolong these conditions rather than lead to improvement or prevention. Not only our penitentiaries and gaols, not only welfare institutions, but also our hospitals, both general and special, are housing many individuals suffering from psychiatric illness and social breakdown, and may indeed be contributing to the social disabilities from which these individuals suffer.

We are encouraged by the increasing public interest in the size and nature of this problem. Governments have historically been involved in mental-health programmes. Most governments are now investing heavily in treatment programmes, in the training of personnel, and the facilitation of research. The Royal Commission on Health Services has given priority to mental-health services, including preventive programmes. Historically, great killers, cholera amongst others, were often reduced and controlled by sanitary measures before their specific causes were known. Some of the great pioneers in public health promoted sanitary organization to control infectious diseases long before Pasteur began the science of bacteriology. The same kind of experimentation in prevention is necessary for mental illness.

Secondary prevention, treatment, is now becoming more widespread and effective and the impact of this on primary prevention may be very great. As we are acting so much on faith and on limited evidence in a complicated situation, we must ensure on-going research to assess our efforts and to evaluate their impact. This is really epidemiological research supported by efforts in the fields of sociology, psychology, and psychiatry. According to Rümke, "the phase in which we are now working may fairly be called 'pre-scientific' – a necessary precursor of more objectively scientific ways of working." (7)

To place primary prevention on a sound basis, many more studies will be necessary. For example, we must know more specifically those symptoms and signs of social or individual breakdown as they occur in any given community. Much will have to be done in the area of "case-finding"; both the public at large and workers in all fields of individual service will require more specific in-depth education regarding psychiatric signs and symptoms. It would also be helpful to develop ways and means of identifying those people in our communities who are vulnerable under conditions of stress and social change; we must understand the mode of action of those "noxious agents" to which they are susceptible.

In the field of public education in mental health, Canada has gained an international reputation. Significant contributions to this field were produced in the early 1920s and 30s, largely sponsored by the Canadian National Committee for Mental Hygiene (now CMHA). Contributors such as Dr. Baruch Silverman and the late Dr. Bert Mitchell of McGill University, the late Dr. William E. Blatz, the late Dr. David Ketchum, and Dr. Roger Myers of the University of Toronto produced pamphlets on child development and parent education which were widely circulated. One of the most prolific writers of articles and materials on positive mental hygiene directed usually to teachers and parents, has been

Dr. S. R. Laycock, Dean Emeritus of the Faculty of Education at the University of Saskatchewan, who has published over 700 such articles. Dr. C. G. Stogdill, presently director of the Child Adjustment Services of the City of Toronto Schools, actively promoted the production and distribution of teaching aids by the federal government. The child training pamphlets, the Ages and Stages series of films, Mental Mechanisms, Symptoms series, and others have proven to be extremely useful. When properly integrated into programmes of public or professional education, they can contribute greatly to the learning process and the development of understanding of the needs of children and adults in our society.

During the post-war years, we have heard much of public health education. Some of our professional education programmes include this as a study area. On the whole, however, practical efforts in public-health education have been spotty and limited. It surely is an important area of concern but not one from which we can anticipate immediate results in direct response to our efforts. Health education programmes can be frustrating for those involved in them and this is particularly so when these programmes are not well supported by other health workers. There can be no doubt of the changes in public attitudes towards mental illness during recent decades. Families, individuals, community agencies, employers, and others are now much more aware of mental illness and more and more they are demanding not only treatment services but efforts to bring these illnesses under control.

On the professional side, these concerns are not new. The term "mental hygiene" was used by an American physician, William Switzer, in 1843. In 1857, in England, there was a proposal for a programme "to promote mental sanitary reform." George Cork of New York State wrote two articles on the promotion of mental health and the prevention of mental illness in 1859. Perhaps one of the most significant contributions was Clifford Beers' autobiography in 1908. In 1909, the United States' National Committee for Mental Hygiene was formed under the leadership of Beers, Adolph Meyer, and William Jones. The Canadian National Committee on Mental Hygiene was founded in Canada in the year 1918. The first president was Dr. Charles F. Martin (professor of medicine at McGill University), the first medical director was Dr. C. K. Clarke (dean of medicine, University of Toronto), and Dr. C. M. Hincks was the executive secretary. Dr. Hincks became medical director in 1924 and held this position until 1952.

There has been concern about the mental health of children and adolescents for over a century. In 1819 there were recommendations for the separation of young offenders from older and more hardened criminals. In 1844, David Francis Condie was urging "moral treatment" of the young. In 1879, Clara T. Leonard said "The younger the child when it enters the family, the more hopeful will be its future life. The longer the child remains in the institution, the greater will be the prospect that it will be a public burden always. In order to bring dependent children at an early age into family life, it will be necessary to pay a small sum for their maintenance for a time, in many cases. Their failure [i.e. institutional children becoming paupers and criminals] is not so much from inherited defects as from the fact that moral stamina has been destroyed by a machine-life, which creates a spirit of dependence and stultifies the affections and moral qualities." (8) In 1899 the first Juvenile Court was established in Chicago – an effort supported by Dr. Adolph Meyer. In 1899 a Dr. Jacobi wrote an article on eugenics, prenatal, natal, and childhood infections, and injuries. In 1921, the Baby Hygiene Association of Boston established a Habit Clinic with Douglas Thorn as the psychiatrist. Since that time there has been a proliferation of child guidance clinics and special institutes, such as the Yale Psycho Clinic and the Institute of Child Studies at the University of Toronto. While much knowledge has been gained regarding child development, it is difficult to identify specific applications of this to date in the area of primary prevention.

Public health is a relatively new profession and one which has gone through very rapid changes in the half century of its formal existence. At the present time, it would be safe to say that major decisions are pending regarding the future professional training and career activities of the public-health professionals. These impending changes seriously complicate our efforts to integrate mental-health activities into public-health programmes. In 1897, Herman Biggs urged the establishment of schools of public health. The first graduate school of public health was founded by Harvard Medical School and Massachusetts Institute of Technology in 1913. The early objectives of training were the control of communicable diseases, environmental sanitation, and elimination of malnutrition. The founders of the school included mental health as a public-health problem from the beginning but developments in this respect were limited. From 1915 to 1935 there were seminars, lectures, and discussions on mental hygiene in the courses on child and maternal health. In 1922, Dr. C. Macfie Campbell covered topics such as mental defects, delinquency, and child guidance. His course included clinical instruction and opportunities were provided for research and advanced work in mental health.

A review of other schools of public health in North America indicates a very similar situation – a stated interest in mental hygiene, a few lectures and seminars, possibly demonstration clinics, and field visits. Since the second world war, however, there has been a marked change; full- and part-time psychiatrists have been appointed to the staff of the schools on a regular basis and there an increasing interest has been shown by the behavioural sciences and the community. The contributions of Lemkau, Caplan, Howell, and others are notable. Not only do the D.P.H. and M.P.H. programmes concern themselves more with mental hygiene but the nature of the course has changed: there is considerable emphasis on the social and community aspects of mental illness, the importance of programme consultants, of early diagnosis, of assessment, and of counselling in all areas. In addition, programmes have been established for other disciplines: mental health courses for nurses, courses in community and administrative psychiatry, courses for mental health consultants, and so on.

It would seem, as Lemkau has often stated, that we have now reached a point where the involvement of public health can contribute much to the increased promotion of mental health and the prevention of psychiatric illnesses. Our task is to provide meaningful involvement of public-health personnel and to demonstrate to them programme areas and methods which they can apply to populations at risk.

It is quite clear that a large part of our programme must be directed towards children. How I wish we really knew how to prevent children from being mentally ill in adult life! In the absence of specific measures, we must surely see that our children are educated in a system which will provide special opportunities for those with special needs and early guidance and treatment for those unable to adjust to the opportunities provided. We must also hope that adequate nutrition, housing, recreation, and work opportunities in later life will help to prevent some of the problems we face. I am greatly encouraged by the increasing concern for children with specific learning disabilities and specific handicaps and the development of special programmes for them; I cannot help but feel that efforts which assist children in overcoming or adjusting to these will have a major impact on their future mental health. Equally, I hope that the increased application of learning theories to children will have the effect of reducing the development of neurotic, psychotic, and character disorders in later life. In urging the establishment of so many specialized services for children and adults, we may be accused of asking for too much. I doubt that we are. If we really value the individual and his health, we cannot ask for less. We must look forward to the day when the promotion and preservation of individual health will be as important as any other activity in our society.

Some fifty years ago, general paresis of the insane – a form of neuro-syphilis – accounted for about 5 per cent of the patients in Canadian mental hospitals. Mastery of syphilis has probably been the most important example of specific primary prevention of a major mental illness. One can also cite pellagra and cretinism as examples. During recent years, it has become apparent that brain injuries related to pregnancy are important factors in mental retardation: eclampsia, asphyxia and actual physical trauma are all capable of affecting the child.

More recently, Rogers, Lilienfeld, and Pasamanick (9) have found that abnormalities of the pre-natal and perinatal periods were significantly associated with behaviour disorders in children. They feel that this finding supports the hypothesis of minimal brain damage. Further preventive measures in the field of obstetrical care relate to the role of German measles in the causation of brain damage as well as deafness or blindness in the child.

All of us in psychiatry have been aware of the effects of recent advances in physical medicine on our field. Everyone is now living longer, including the mentally retarded and mentally ill. Certainly the increase in longevity means many more people are developing cerebral arteriosclerosis and senile psychosis – this increase is quite apparent in the admission rates to and populations of our mental hospitals.

I do not propose to deal in any detail with specific measures at this time but would refer those of you who are interested to chapter 3, "Mental Disorders of Known Etiology," in the APHA Manual, *Mental Disorders: A Guide to Control Methods.*

In psychiatric illness, indeed in all illnesses, we are aware of somatic, psychological, and social aspects. In primary prevention it is becoming increasingly clear that no single technique, no single programme can deal effectively with all of these aspects. Lemkau summarizes the present situation as follows (10):

programs to prevent the mental illnesses . . . must depend upon which mental illness or kind of mental illness is to be prevented. . . . there appear to be no ways in which the human being can become ill that do not also induce or cause changes in behaviour which, if severe enough, may amount to mental illness . . . infection can cause delirium – underdosage of hormones can produce cretinism – diabetes results from insulin deficiency – uncontrolled diabetes speeds up arterio-sclerosis which sometimes leads to difficulties of memory and other mental symptoms – new growths can cause mental illness either directly or indirectly – inadequate vitamins cause pellagra – genetic errors cause pku. . . .

Ideas and feelings are considered by some to cause symptoms of mental illness – in this area much can be done through the familiar resources of education and management of the environment. . . . Why don't parents teach children how to live? – the harm done to individuals by understimulation. . . .

As there are many mental illnesses, there will have to be many different programs of prevention. Some of these will deal with the chemistry and physics of the body and some with ideas and feelings. Some will supply stimulation to maximize health. These types are currently being tried on a scale more massive than has ever before been attempted. Some are directed toward alleviating the poignancy of debilitating conscious or unconscious conflict. Prevention of the mental illnesses cannot be conceived, and should not be spoken of, as a single program for a single disease; rather, all should strive toward multiple programs with objectives as specific as can be shown to be worthy in the light of what is known at the time action is needed and becomes possible. I venture to predict that the future of the prevention of the mental illnesses will include an even larger series of models upon which action programs can be based than I have been able to lay before you, and that there will, through our determination, be more people to work at the job and more money to hire them.

REFERENCES

1. LEMKAU, P. V. Prospects for the prevention of mental illnesses. *Ment. Hyg.*, 1966, 50:172–79.
2. BLOOM, B. L. The "medical model," miasma theory and community mental health. *Commun. Ment. Hlth J.*, 1965, 1:333–38.
3. In GALDSTON, I. (Ed.). *Social Medicine: Its Deviations and Objectives.* New York: Commonwealth Fund, 1949.
4. PROGRAM AREA COMMITTEE ON MENTAL HEALTH. *Mental Disorders: A Guide to Control Methods.* New York: American Public Health Association, 1962.
5. UNITED STATES DEPARTMENT OF HEALTH, EDUCATION AND WELFARE. *The Prevention of Disability in Mental Disorders.* Mental Health Monograph no. 1. Public Health Service Publication no. 924. Washington: Government Printing Office, 1962.
6. KRAFT, I. Preventing mental ill health in early childhood. *Ment. Hyg.*, 1964, 48: 413–23.
7. In SODDY, K. and R. H. AHRENFELDT (Eds.). *Mental Health in a Changing World.* Philadelphia: J. B. Lippincott, 1965.
8. In *Mental Health Teaching in Schools of Public Health.* A report of a conference at Arden House, New York, held in 1959. New York: Columbia University Press, 1961.
9. ROGERS, M. E., A. M. LILIENFELD, and B. PASAMANICK. Pre-natal and peri-natal factors in the development of childhood behaviour disorders. *Acta Psychiatrica Scandinavica*, suppl. 102, 1955: Pregnancy experience and the development of behaviour disorder in children. *Amer. J. Psychiat.*, 1956, 112:613–18.
10. LEMKAU, P. V. Prevention in psychiatry: Is there such a thing? *Amer. J. publ. Hlth*, 1965, 55:554–60.

2 The Role of Treatment and Rehabilitation

In 1964, the Regional Office for Europe of the World Health Organisation sponsored a seminar on Public Health Practice and the Prevention of Mental Illness. The report of this seminar (1) discusses the pros and cons of giving mental hygienists training different from that for psychiatry, the close relationship between preventive and therapeutic work, the role of professionals from other than the mental-health field, and the need for organizational patterns to be individually tailored to local needs. It is clear that all of those involved in treatment and rehabilitation should also be involved in promotion and prevention because, at this time, treatment and rehabilitation may provide the best opportunity for influencing and changing attitudes in a manner conducive to those social changes which will be increasingly necessary if the population at large is to be protected from many noxious social influences.

The third, fifth, and other reports of the technical committees on mental health of the World Health Organisation support the community psychiatric hospital or centre as the focal point of all mental-health programmes, including prevention. When consideration is given to the extent of psychiatric morbidity, it may well be that the most effective and extensive opportunities for positive prevention rest in a close relationship with the co-ordinated mental-health services of the community. In these centres patients can be treated and the effects of their illnesses on other members of the family and the community minimized; contact with relatives and friends may influence and change attitudes; through work with social agencies, employers, the clergy, the police, and others further constructive changes may be possible; and by having the centre in the community, related to and part of the community, the separation and stigmatization of mental illness and the mentally ill may be further reduced.

In this connection it is essential to consider the role of voluntary organizations in the mental health field. Why voluntary agencies? The government provides and directs most mental-health services. Why should private citizens devote their time and energy to this problem of mental health and mental illness? The government has accepted responsibility for mental illness and the problems can safely be left to the government. These questions are largely answered by the history of health services. Here the evidence is overwhelming. Whenever and in whichever area you wish to choose, you will find that health services have grown and flourished where public interest and support and participation were keen. Where public apathy and disinterest and lack of co-operation existed, health services have lagged the most. The history of mental-health services illustrates this point most effectively.

Experience demonstrates that health services do not develop spontaneously. Yet it is very difficult to legislatively create high standards of health care. In general, health services stem from concerted, vigorous, and continuing effort on the part of public-spirited citizens who, once convinced of the worthiness of their cause, carry on the battle for recognition despite any and all setbacks. This is one of the most important roles of active, healthy, voluntary organizations.

When this kind of community support is not available, programmes are almost foredoomed and will never be as effective as they should be. While this point may be overstated, it is basic and fundamental to every development related to mental health services.

Advances in the mental health field have been significant because of co-operation between federal and provincial governments and voluntary agencies. All of these derive their support from the general public. Before this support can be mobilized, there has to be public understanding and acceptance of the problems of mental illness and the promotion of mental health, the willingness to face up to its full meaning in terms of the national well-being and economy, the drain on the country's health and wealth in both the narrowest and widest sense of these terms.

It is in developing such support that the voluntary organization in the mental-health field stands or falls. Here it has its most important role to play, dispelling misunderstandings and prejudices and replacing them with the awareness and attitudes which alone can pave the way for advance against our most serious public-health threat. The voluntary organization has been and must continue to be the pioneer in the mental-health field with its educational and informational programme. As a citizen group its strength must result from its closeness to the community. It has no political, religious, or racial axe to grind and its motives should be beyond reproach. As such, it is in a particularly preferred position to spread understanding about mental health, to inform the public about the basic principles that may be applied in everyday living: that mental health isn't something that one either has or has not but that it can be improved and strengthened and, conversely, weakened and allowed to run down; that most mental illnesses are gradual processes which if detected in good time can receive medical attention giving the patient a good chance of recovery and avoiding long-term serious illness and hospitalization; that there are specially trained people available to help in these cases; that mental health does not belong to a separate compartment from the rest of our lives but is closely tied up with our physical well-being, social way of life, church ties, family relationships, how we work and play, and how we get along with our friends and neighbours in community living. Simple facts? Certainly! And yet how much treasure of health and purse could be saved if these facts were known and understood and made part and parcel of everyday life!

The voluntary organization can be the most effective agency in changing community attitudes along such lines because it is both in and of the community. The parent, clergyman, teacher, employer, and family doctor are surely in the best position to maintain community mental health and it is their continuous awareness of such responsibility and practice of sound mental-health principles which will ultimately reduce the size of this problem. These are usually key people in the local voluntary mental-health organizations which, by thus representing the major groups in the community, can keep this awareness active. By carefully planned programmes year in and year out they are able to help translate sound principles into constructive action. This transformation from facts known to attitudes lived is the only real measure of accomplishment in any public-health field. This essential grass-roots progress is simply not possible for government at any level to achieve, however well intentioned it might be. Certainly government has its part in the over-all picture and fortunately in Canada our governments are increasingly aware of and active in this field. But it is most important that we keep our thinking clear concerning the respective roles, and that the areas of responsibility remain well-defined.

The voluntary group which launches itself into community mental-health programmes has a very real job to do. The courage, alertness, ingenuity and, I am sure, patience, of its members will most assuredly be tested. The association will run into a don't-care apathy on the part of many who either don't know or won't face some of the unpleasant facts. In addition to this kind of passive resistance, there will be the active antagonism of others who may be only too aware of the facts and see a threat to their comfortable routine or even to their security.

Resistances based on shame, fear, and ignorance are the usual hazards for the course of a mental health association. It will find that its good intentions are often questioned, that every argument advanced for its continuance may be met by a dozen against it. It will be disheartened at the paradox of people seemingly not wanting to be helped. There will be – isn't there always? – the lack of sufficient funds.

And yet, because the voluntary organization plays such a needed part in the mental-health programme, it grows in strength as its mettle is tested again and again. The public must be informed and attitudes implanted and nourished. At this point it will find that information and education are not enough, that they are just the start. It must be directed to action – the kind of action that follows when people realize that their resources and facilities to cope with the psychiatric illnesses and their prevention are grossly inadequate.

Only then will the groundswell of public opinion break through barriers and resistance. The shortages and the inadequacies will be overcome. Mental-health clinics, general hospital psychiatric wards, facilities for the mentally retarded, rehabilitation services for the delinquent and the alcoholic, come into being and there is a new look in the whole community mental-health programme. Research into prevention and treatment and community problems will be advanced. This is not a theoretical concept. It is taking place right across Canada. Not perhaps of the order you and I would like to see but certainly, compared with what was happening a few short years ago, an encouraging amount has been accomplished.

You will have noticed that I have not yet mentioned the mental hospital. I feel that these hospitals require special consideration. These institutions have been isolated as though they harboured infectious diseases rather than being hospitals doing their best under the most difficult conditions to cure mentally sick persons. They are in great need of help from the communities they serve. Even here resistance will be met and must be overcome.

The general hospitals have traditionally made excellent use of voluntary organizations in carrying out recreational and educational programmes, entertainments, running canteens, dances, concerts, etc.

The mental hospitals not only need such similar services but would actually derive more benefit from this community participation because of the very nature of the illnesses they treat. The voluntary organization which comes into the mental hospital is giving the patients much more than a mere show or service. The warmth of human contact and sympathetic attention are the very essence of the curative approach to mental illness. The mental patient's need for hospital treatment, which includes contact with normal community life and help in re-adjustment to post-hospital life, can only be met by teamwork of hospital and community. When we think of volunteer services to a hospital we think usually of the community person who comes to the hospital to visit wards, sponsor parties, bring entertainment and other similar activities. The broader view is that of a joint hospital-community responsibility to spread understanding of mental illness, help meet the needs of discharged patients, train volunteers, make community leaders a part of hospital plans and programmes and make available the best possible treatment for hospitalized members of the communities the hospital serves. This link with the community has been so effectively demonstrated in many places that I feel it is only a matter of time until every mental institution will have it as part of its normal operation.

With this contact the voluntary association develops a bond of sympathy between the community and the mental hospital. The veiled mystery, the whispers, and the rumours are dispelled and the hospital brought out of its fear-inspiring isolation. The people in the community get to know something of the problems facing the hospital administrators and also come to know of the very valuable work being done in our hospitals by capable and conscientious staff members. When an increased budget is sought for additional staff, building renovation, or new equipment, there is a powerful voice added to the request of the hospital administrator – the expressed support of the community for a better hospital – and the project is brought nearer to reality.

The patients are helped by the community which shows its concern for them while they are in hospital. They can be helped even more by a society sympathetic to their needs when discharge day comes around. The voluntary association can lead the way in providing this type of service – assistance in the rehabilitation process, getting resettled in the home, and in employment. This activity flourishes best, of course, in a community climate that has been made friendly towards and knowledgeable about former mental patients.

And while on the subject of mental hospitals, I would like to leave a few thoughts with you. First of all, a truly functional mental hospital must be a community hospital. As such, the concept of a geographically or psychologically isolated institution miles away from the nearest community is outdated. It puts a barrier of distance between itself and the community which is not only bad for the patients but is undoubtedly one of the factors making it difficult to attract professional and auxiliary staff. Again, what about the size of our mental hospitals? Can the best treatment programme be carried on in an institution which houses several thousand patients? I am inclined to believe that in future planning smaller psychiatric services situated in concentrated population areas will receive increasing attention. They would be associated with active treatment hospitals easily accessible to the community and attractive to staff personnel. They would provide facilities for day care, operate out-patient departments, and profitably participate in the total health service of the community. Their close integration in community health programming would, I am sure, be a factor warmly welcomed by mental-health associations who would find their task appreciably lightened by such a relationship. The more remote hospitals could be used for longer treatment programmes or custodial care, as required, after investigation and treatment in the centre near home.

Another field in which the voluntary mental-health association can do valuable work is geriatrics. Our mental hospitals are overcrowded with the older age-group. Here is a challenge for a preventive programme to decrease the amount of mental illness among older people. It is a particularly complicated problem and involves the understanding of industry, social agencies, unions, health agencies, and government. The Canadian Mental Health Association is already doing some very fine work in this field and I hope that it can find time to increase and expand this valuable contribution to the mental health of our country.

The mentally retarded members of our population also pose a major challenge. Many of the important questions involved have not yet been answered by our professional research workers. Among such questions are: Which of the retarded should be cared for at home and which in an institution? What is the effect of a retarded child on other members of the family? Special school classes are available for certain types of retarded children and it is obvious that much can be done to assist this group. Another group obviously requires institutional care and more of these institutions are being developed. A third group apparently can be looked after effectively in special classes sponsored by community groups with the assistance of educational and health agencies. Voluntary bodies are achieving some highly satisfactory results across Canada by developing parent groups which stress training and social adjustment opportunities for these children.

Recently, while speaking to a group of fellow psychiatrists, I said "We, like other physicians, must be concerned with treatment, rehabilitation, and prevention. Our primary qualification is in medicine and treatment – from this work and research will come our programmes of prevention. Training in medicine and psychiatry does not qualify us as experts or even as the professionals best qualified to deal with prevention of psychiatric illness or the promotion of better mental health." I believe that recognition of the psychiatrist's basic qualifications is essential for the development of psychiatric treatment services under central auspices has encouraged the development of preventive programmes under the same auspices with the result that the community anticipates separate action with regard to the prevention of psychiatric illness rather than its inclusion in a total community public health programme.

I should like to make some suggestions regarding community services for the treatment and prevention of psychiatric illnesses and for the promotion of mental health:

1. The development of isolated services for psychiatric patients should, in general, be discouraged.

2. Services for psychiatric patients should be fully integrated at all levels with those provided for other illnesses.

3. Public health services should accept in a meaningful way the concept of a whole person – the soma and the psyche. Thus case detection, control, and follow-up of psychiatric illness should be of as much concern to public health as are programmes to prevent maternal mortality, infant mortality, tuberculosis, and so on.

Dr. Gerald Caplan of Harvard University states that secondary and tertiary prevention are possible at this time. In illnesses of psychological and social etiology – as we understand such illnesses at the present time – primary prevention may be possible but, to quote Caplan, "this relates to communities and not to individual children – reducing the rate of mental disorders in a population of children and not prevention of mental disorders in a particular child." There seems to be general agreement that there are certain general rules of health and that adequate education and recreation will reduce the total volume of mental illness in children and adults.

The development of isolated facilities should be discouraged as they are inefficient and over-emphasize psychiatry to the detriment of the patient. Paediatricians and other physicians should be much more involved in the supervision and treatment of children with psychiatric disorders with the psychiatrist assuming a consultant role. It is unlikely that we will see a significant increase in the ratio of child psychiatrists to population in the near future and our problems will continue as at present until we find successful ways of involving other physicians. A further disadvantage of isolated services is the way in which they stigmatize and identify a child as being mentally ill. Because of this we are faced with demands for the development of a continuum of services under psychiatric auspices rather than the provision of service to these children through the same agencies and arrangements as are provided for other children. A psychiatric service in a welfare agency or a public health service is, from this point of view, an isolated service – psychiatric service should be provided for such agencies as are other medical services.

Psychiatric services for both children and adults – diagnosis, treatment, and rehabilitation – should be fully integrated with other health services. This is not to deny the need for the development of certain highly specialized services but to emphasize that the family physician, the paediatrician, the paediatric and psychiatric service of the general hospital should be the first line of defence and the child should only be removed from this stream when it is necessary to have special services. At the present time, we separate almost all such cases from the usual stream and, as a result, every new clinic has a waiting list and an overwhelming continuing treatment load almost as quickly as it is organized.

Public health services should accept responsibility for the prevention of psychiatric illness and the promotion of mental health as they do for most illnesses. I said earlier "in a meaningful way" because we do not as yet have many specific environmental factors to consider nor do we know specifically what action to take to strengthen the host against psychiatric illnesses. We are, however, increasingly aware of the importance of parental attitudes towards pregnancy, of the importance of the mother-child relationship, of our relationships to the community in which we live – its mores and its social structure – and of the value of anticipatory guidance and counselling.

We must, each one of us in the health, education, and welfare services, face up to our own value systems, our attitudes, and even our own prejudices. Medical treatment may take place at three levels – somatic, psychological, and social – and in this respect psychiatry is not qualitatively different from other branches of medicine. It is, however, quantitatively different. We have relatively few somatic treatments – we place great emphasis on psychological and social factors. In the past seventy-five years or so medicine has become preoccupied with specific treatments; symptomatic treatment has been down-graded, only specific treatments, either medical or surgical, are considered worthwhile. To talk to patients is to do nothing; we must order a treatment. In the development of a psychiatric programme and the promotion of mental health this process must be reversed. To participate fully in a psychotherapeutic or counselling role, one must continuously increase one's understanding of oneself, of one's own reactions, and one's own attitudes: only through this process can we hope to help those who are having to find ways of adapting to their environment. Is it not true that most of us feel initially uncomfortable in a counselling role; to listen, to interpret, and to allow the patient to work through a problem goes against the grain; we feel we should be doing something. How often we create problems for ourselves by trying to solve someone else's dilemma! Very often such non-directive counselling is the most appropriate treatment: to allow an expectant mother to talk through her problem, to find her own solution, rather than to move in with or without the husband to find a solution for her. All of us have our own reality – the world as we perceive it – all of us have our own goals, ambitions, and phantasies and many of our problems relate to the way in which we find solutions rather than to the solutions themselves. Acceptance of the similarities and differences between physical and mental health and of the importance of self-understanding is of the essence in the development of a comprehensive mental-health programme. It has become easy to accept mental health and mental illness at an intellectual level but not so at an emotional level. I have heard ardent speakers pleading for the acceptance of children who have recovered from mental illness; but I have then found that the speaker himself would not accept such a former patient and that the residential centre in which the patient had been accommodated prior to illness had a policy prohibiting the admission of such children. The attitude seems to be: "Others should do it; I accept the need intellectually, but if I did anything about it it might cause problems for me." If the need were fully accepted the emotional preparation for dealing with the problem would exist. Many people express the need for a preventive mental-health programme while completely rejecting all the tenets of mental health. Thus the acceptance of such tenets by senior administrative personnel is an absolute necessity in the development of a mental-health programme.

If mental-health programmes are to be integrated with other health programmes, action must be carried forward by other than mental-health personnel. Public health will be involved in primary prevention (as it is now), case finding, promotion, and follow-up. Treatment should be provided through the usual channels of private practice, o.p.d.'s, and special facilities. In general, treatment should not be provided through clinics attached to public health agencies, social-service agencies, or the schools – such a method of organization may be the most desirable in a given instance but only if it does not reduce the kind of integration which appears to be necessary at this time. The establishment of mental-health treatment services under these various auspices has minimized other activities which should be fostered in the development of a preventive programme. While it is realized that this is not invariably so, in general the staff of such clinics have been used to provide individual service, thus limiting the time available for programme consultation, staff development, and consultation with other professional workers who should continue to provide direct service to patients. There are relatively few well-baby clinics whose staff has been appropriately trained to be aware of emotional development or which have available to them consultant nurses, social workers, psychologists, or psychiatrists with adequate psychiatric experience to provide comprehensive in-service training in this respect. With relatively few exceptions, this is also true in universities, schools, and social agencies and yet the real hope at the moment is to provide a total milieu which will permit healthy development. It is quite possible that psychology, social work, psychiatry, and other disciplines could provide constructive consultation in programme development but at present their main involvement appears to be at the level of problem-solving of cases. The number of cases requiring treatment appears to be almost without limit; is it not time to recognize that a solution will not be found through the development of more and more clinics but rather through a comprehensive programme in the planning of which social and psychological needs would be considered as carefully as are physical needs.

Repeatedly, during my visits to mental-health services, the matter of training for personnel to direct community mental-health programmes has come up. To date, there has been a tendency to seek out a well-qualified clinician, most likely with interest and experience in children's work, and then expect him to develop a local programme. The local programmes as a rule are based on a number of very general statements which cannot be made concrete and which are too abstract to be meaningful to the majority of people. As these physicians have not had any experience or training in administration or community consultation, they do not know how to proceed. It appears that too many individuals are now being asked to assume responsibilities for which they are not prepared – they are learning through experience – whereas there is a great deal of knowledge about administration, organization, and consultation which could be taught and which would greatly facilitate the work of our mental-health services.

The increased emphasis on community mental-health programmes rather than traditional mental-hospital services has led to an increasing number and variety of programmes aimed at involving the local community. It is hoped that involvement of the local communtiy will make these services more meaningful to its members and that they will be more closely related to or a part of general health service. Experience to date would indicate that fulfilment of this plan is extremely difficult. The pros and cons of a close relationship with the welfare services, the educational services, and the forensic services must also be considered as we find in these services many factors which could contribute to a mental-health programme.

If we really want to integrate and co-ordinate mental-health programmes with other health programmes, we must consider the relationship of mental-health services to public-health services and to general health services such as the local physicians, general hospital, and so on. This is the one area where our programmes are presently most confusing to other health authorities and to the public at large as there is an almost universal tendency to feel that mental-health services should be developed on their own, the notable exception to that rule being the rapid development of psychiatric services in general hospitals although even here there are many problems of organization and communication and much isolation persists.

It is clear that there is now a major commitment to "community" psychiatry. I cannot do better than quote from a paper given by Dr. R. O. Jones at the eighteenth Mental Hospital Institute in Boston recently:

Even if it could be shown that the community mental health model is the best model for the immediate care of psychiatric patients, are there possibilities of other harmful effects which demand consideration? Obviously there are. One of these has to do with our genetic hypothesis. There is no doubt that the birth rate to schizophrenic women, living outside the mental hospital, according to modern practice, is significantly higher than those of a generation ago, when most schizophrenics were confined. If there is anything in the genetic theory of schizophrenia, then this kind of statistic must be taken with some seriousness. One of my staff has suggested that what we really need is "Stelovid" – a combination of Stelazine and Enovid. If there is nothing in the genetic theory and schizophrenia and other behaviour disturbances are largely environmental, then we equally have to ask the question (and it is being asked more and more these days), concerning the effects on the rest of the family and particularly on the children in returning them to the care of the schizophrenic parent. The Maudsley Hospital reports that children coming into their children's department are three times more likely to have a mentally ill parent than those with a matched background – the control group coming from the local school systems. Seymour Kety, addressing this Institute a year ago, pointed out that we really did not know a satisfactory etiology or treatment for any of the major psychoses and reviewed promising leads from the biochemical fields. He warned then against an exclusive pre-occupation with community concepts leading to neglect of research and of action in the biochemical and physiological fields.

A good deal of our success in community psychiatry has come about because of such treatment agents as electroconvulsive therapy and drug therapy. Particularly in a period of tight money and restricted personnel, it seems to me that we are in danger of neglecting other promising lines of development if we unhesitatingly feel that present trends in community mental health provide all the answers.

A set of further negative effects, possibly stemming from our enthusiasm for community psychiatry, are commented upon by H. Warren Dunham. Dunham suggests that some feel that psychiatry is being utilised to move us closer in the direction of the welfare state. He says that this may not be an undesirable thing in itself – I personally feel that it is undesirable – but certainly I would agree with Dunham that if we are going in this direction, we should be aware of the role that we are asked to play. Already, certainly, the doctor/patient relationship has not been preserved as much in many forms of psychiatry as it has been in other areas of medicine, despite the fact that most of us would argue that the doctor/patient relationship has traditionally been the thing which psychiatrists have been most skilled in. I would agree with Dunham that we have created some distrust in our medical colleagues' minds. To me it seems that some of the movement to community psychiatry perpetuates the old state-control system and in effect is no more than changing the location of the state hospital from its present location to the centre of the community. The same outmoded and, I would believe, unhappy administrative arrangements come along too. Many community centres are staffed by full-time state-employed physicians. It may be that these people are able to mingle more freely with community social agencies, schools, etc. but, in many instances, I do not believe that they mingle any more freely with the medical community or are more involved in other medical facilities. One of the goals enunciated by President Kennedy in promulgating the community psychiatric programme was "to bring psychiatry back into the main stream of medicine". In some areas the community mental health centre is certainly not accomplishing this particular objective. Immediately two objections to this model are raised. The first has to do with the team – where do our valued allies in the paramedical fields fit in? Despite the fact that we seem to be able to treat a fair number of people in the private practice of psychiatry without ancillary help, it is probable that when the total population is insured, we will get into the social classes where the need is greater. Certainly, then social work, psychological testing, occupational therapy, vocational rehabilitation and so on will all be important. We would feel, however, that many other areas in medicine will do exactly the same thing and that again the patient with chronic heart disease is frequently in as much need of social workers as the patient with chronic schizophrenia. Surely, however, we do not have to keep a section of the population medically indigent and have them treated by salaried physicians in order to give them the benefits of psychological or social service help. Therefore, we would hope that these other professions would organise themselves in such a way that they will be available to work in partnership with the physicians of the community to provide a total care plan and that with this re-organisation they can take responsibility in their area of competence. The second objection has to do with the preventive aspect of psychiatry. How can the non-medical preventative aspects of the community centre be incorporated? What happens with the schools, child guidance clinics, and so on? Again, we do not believe that these offer insurmountable difficulties. Psychiatrists who spend the major part of their time in this type of community practice may act in a consulting basis for a sessional indemnity. There may be, of course, some psychiatrists who will want to spend all their time in this area and it has been suggested that just as we have public health men in other areas of medicine to look after the preventative group aspects, so we should have public health psychiatrists to do the same thing.

I cannot help but feel that the first essential in the development of a positive mental health programme is a consideration of the psychological development of the human being. While recognising that psychological function cannot be separated from physical function, it is equally clear to quote Lemkau that "Every model of pathological process produces diseases that have psychiatric symptoms. Preventive psychiatry is an inevitable component of all disease prevention and every physician has a role as preventor of psychiatric illnesses. Regardless of how narrow his concept of his specialty, he cannot avoid this role". It might be added that every stress to which an individual is exposed demands a psychological adaptation. Thus, all individuals engaged in the helping professions – physician, nurse, school teacher, psychologist, social worker, occupational therapist, clergy, guidance personnel, etc. should have a fundamental and clear understanding of psychological development and adaptation to stress. This knowledge should not be limited to theoretical considerations or didactic lectures but must, to be meaningful, be taught through demonstration in the various settings to which people turn for help.

Certain steps have been taken in the broader field of public health to introduce control programmes for cancer, crippled children, and others where specific causes are not known. These programmes are based on certain principles which psychiatrists generally have not yet accepted. The principles behind these more recent programmes seem to involve arrangements which will ensure adequate diagnosis, adequate therapy, and adequate follow-up. This assumes an ability to develop and a willingness to accept standards, adjusted from time to time in the light of available knowledge, of adequate diagnosis, adequate therapy, and adequate follow-up.

At this point it might be as well to mention the matter of confidentiality which seems to be stressed so frequently by those who object to a case register which is a necessary base for any control programme in the health field. The main objection seems to be that psychiatry deals with more personal, more intimate, and potentially more harmful material than is found in the field of physical illness and this is probably a valid statement. On the other hand, the operation of a case index is not dependent on the availabilty of such confidential material. In the initial stages, all that is necessary is identification data, diagnosis, treatment, and follow-up services. If it appears that a patient has not received an adequate diagnostic work-up, then arrangements can be made with the patient's personal physician or other agency to see that such is done and the same principles would apply to treatment and follow-up. It might also be pointed out that welfare agencies dealing with very similar content to that found in psychiatric services have pioneered the development of the social-service index which has proved to be of inestimable value in the development of more adequate welfare services.

In connection with a control programme, one would also have to deal with the fetish presently popular regarding voluntary treatment. In our desire to rid ourselves of the legal restraints and controls developed in the past to protect patients and the community, we have allowed ourselves to lose perspective and we fail to recognize that in all health programmes it is necessary to have certain sanctions which can be applied. When we wish to control infectious diseases, we use quarantine and isolation; if we believe that mental health should be subject to a control programme we must retain certain sanctions. There is increasing, although not yet firm, evidence that many individuals may act as precipitating or associated causes of mental illness and/or aggressivity in other people; the day may come when quarantine of these individuals will be socially necessary. The recently developed programmes in the field of alcoholism are also having to face this problem. As programmes become effective in the treatment of those alcoholics who are prepared to participate in treatment, the problem of alcoholics who lack insight or sufficient controls to undergo treatment voluntarily becomes more pressing. More and more frequently these programmes make reference to the desirability of sanctions which would enable them to treat this latter group of patients. To be realistic about the voluntary care of patients, what we really want is to have a programme where that which is medically indicated can be carried out. In the general health field, there is really no such thing as a voluntary self-admission; the patient's doctor recommends admission to hospital or to an out-patient service and the patient or guardian consents to this. This should also be the case when we are dealing with psychiatric illnesses. Our preoccupation with voluntary services may well fail to provide adequate protection for the patient and the community and it is necessary at this point to indicate the need for a proper assessment of this matter.

In an effort to bridge the gap between the major personal care programmes (that is health, education, and welfare), a number of programmes have developed a special group of people variously known as mental-health consultants, liaison officers, teacher-psychologists, and so on, whose primary function is to establish effective liaison between psychiatric and other services. Through this liaison it is felt that the supportive services will gain increased skills in caring for people who do not need specific psychiatric treatment and the whole matter of referrals and liaison between specific health services and these other services should be much improved. The development of such groups seems to be one of the most worthwhile innovations during recent years, for it should enable those in non-psychiatric services to care for a considerable number of patients with psychiatric symptoms and thus reduce the demand for specific psychiatric therapy. But this effort to increase the abilities of people in the general-health field, educational services, welfare, and forensic services, while very worthwhile, has a potential danger which must be considered. All of these other services are designed for specific purposes and the people therein have definite roles to fill. It is not inconceivable that school teachers, law enforcement personnel and others, might become psycho-therapists rather than continuing in their proper role. Such a change of roles could seriously jeopardize adequate essential services which are not only socially necessary but can contribute in a proper supportive way to mental-health programmes if they are fulfilling their own objectives properly. It is necessary to emphasize that the ability of a teacher to handle normal children effectively, to understand human development, and to allow for individual variations is quite different from undertaking the treatment of a very sick child in an ordinary classroom situation. There is good reason to think that much of the criticism of our efforts to introduce mental health activities into schools and other areas of social life exists because we do confuse these roles. It is perhaps not too early for mental-health personnel to stress the necessity for professional workers in other fields to maintain their proper social roles while learning to understand normal human development, individual variations, and the need to work effectively with individuals wherever they happen to be.

The community mental-health services to date seem, consciously or otherwise, to have avoided two very pressing problems. Firstly, whether we like it or not, the major problems insofar as the community is concerned are presented by the occupants of institutional facilities, namely, the psychotic mentally ill, the mentally defective, the aged, the chronically ill, the delinquent, and the social misfit. In this connection, one cannot help but recognize the very real problem of providing adequate assistance for people of all age groups when a psychiatric emergency occurs. There are at least two important areas of psychiatric emergency. In the adult, psychiatric emergencies develop which demand, for the protection either of the patient or the community, hospitalization as quickly as possible. To date the most effective programme for coping with this is that in Amsterdam under the direction of Professor Querido. Many other communitities are now attempting to develop this important type of service. Such an emergency service for adults is indeed essential and the necessary element appears to be the provision of a central agency from which emergency help can always be obtained on a 24-hour, 7-day basis, and which has access to information about patients and their previous treatment as well as to treatment services so that immediate consultations and admissions can be arranged as necessary.

Efforts to provide emergency consultation have been accompanied by the development and popularization of crisis therapy. Individuals and families are continuously adjusting to change which, not uncommonly, seems to provoke psychiatric illness. There are a number of possible outcomes for these crises: some individuals find a solution for the problem without help; some indulge in a search for a solution – drugs, LSD, etc.; others act out; a certain number are seen to be mentally ill and help is sought from medical-psychiatric sources. The psychiatric services at this time can present the model of change and crisis without establishing a model of illness or anticipation of continuing disability. Such crisis activity can do much to prevent the social breakdown syndrome which is a concomitant of the social deprivation which frequently accompanies illness. Dr. Leopold Bellak of New York, speaking at the 1967 annual meeting of the Ontario Psychiatric Association, described the role and nature of brief and emergency psychotherapy in much the same manner.

The second group of emergencies are those which concern children. These are not usually as dramatic or acute in the time sense as are adult emergencies. There are, however, a large number of cases where it is obvious that the family or other placement is about to distintegrate unless rapid steps are taken to introduce treatment. It is noteworthy that a number of child guidance agencies, while continuing to provide the traditional type of child guidance service where this is indicated, are also becoming more flexible in making arrangements for a rapid assessment and disposal of emergency cases. The local mental-health services must arrange such emergency care for children or they will not be fulfilling their role adequately.

Secondly, many community mental-health services seem to be unduly concerned with the stigma related to psychiatric hospitals. They seem to feel that involvement in the after-care of discharged patients or in the assessment and disposal of cases prior to admission will seriously jeopardize their other efforts in the community. There is good reason to think that such is not the case and that communities will not think of mental-health services as being truly effective so long as they leave the community to face many of these problems without the professional assistance they expect and should obtain from community psychiatric services.

It is also apparent that proper functioning of a community mental-health service as a referral agency will further illustrate the undesirable aspects of existing laws having to do with mental illness. It does seem time for these laws to be changed in a way which, while protecting the rights of the individual patient, will provide for the treatment of mental illness on the basis of medical judgment rather than legalistic procedures.

The present situation, in which one to one therapeutic techniques are employed, also requires consideration. Whether this form of treatment be called psychotherapy, counselling, interviewing, case work, or some other euphemism, it must be clear that all people, all patients, all children, have a need for a relationship with one person to whom they can turn with confidence and with the assurance of understanding and acceptance and who will help them with their reality testing and problems. The present status and over-concern with intrinsic psycho-dynamic problems may well be leaving many people without this relationship and perhaps the establishment of this relationship is the greatest role a social worker, nurse, or psychiatrist can fill. There is reason to believe that the establishment of such a relationship will accomplish more in the areas of prevention at all levels than will an over-concern with the intrinsic psycho-dynamic problems of the thousands of patients now being treated by psychiatric services every year. As it is logistically impossible to provide these thousands of patients with effective psycho-dynamically oriented therapy, this form of treatment should be left for those selected patients for whom it can be beneficial and should be seen as providing us with understandings which can be used in the development of the supportive type of treatment which is implied in the statement "the need for a relationship with one person to whom he can turn with confidence and with the assurance of understanding and acceptance."

In many ways the contents of this presentation may be seen as negative. Such is not the intent. Mental health and psychiatry should not be seen as an isolated problem but as part of a whole; surely the prevention of childhood and adult mental illness must be a responsibility of public health. More progress will be made if programmes to accomplish this are organized in the same manner as are programmes to deal with other illnesses.

My concerns may be naive. In our sophisticated age we have a tendency to discuss basic issues and then move forward to develop more and more services without solving any of the problems of co-ordination and integration. Everyone is agreed that co-ordination, integration, and regionalization are basic needs provided that they themselves are not to be co-ordinated or restricted in any way. I suggest that this is a core problem facing all health, welfare, and education services at this time.

As a conclusion to this paper, I would like to quote Dr. Carstairs: "I should like to point out that psycho-analysis gives especial prominence to one element in the treatment of mental disorders which has long been part of good psychiatric practice – which is, indeed, as old as the Hippocratic Oath; namely, the relationship of mutual respect between doctor and patient, the readiness to help and (when volition is lost) the readiness to accept help. There is no statistical proof that sincerity and humanity in one's dealing with people in need will influence their future mental health; but this is an act of faith which I, and many others, have no difficulty in making." (2)

REFERENCES

1. *Seminar on Public Health Practice and the Prevention of Mental Illness,* held at London, July 6–17, 1964. Copenhagen: World Health Organisation Regional Office for Europe, 1965. Pp. 2, 3, 4.
2. CARSTAIRS, G. M. Preventive psychiatry: Is there such a thing? *J. ment. Sci.,* 1958, 104.

3 Primary Prevention: Is it Possible Now?

It is quite clear that a programme for the control of psychiatric disorders is possible now. And not only is it possible but the nature and extent of psychiatric illnesses will soon make such a programme mandatory. It appears that we in Canada are committed to the control of psychiatric disorders through the full integration of psychiatric services with other health services: that is, medical care, hospital care, and public health. Is primary prevention possible now? The answer appears to be an affirmative one.

The development of programmes for primary prevention will require a clear recognition of the inadequacies as well as the possibilities of our present knowledge. Developments in this area must not be deferred because of the inadequacy of present knowledge, rather efforts must be made to prevent disorders and promote mental health. To the maximum extent possible, these efforts should be accompanied by research programmes which will, at this stage, be as much concerned with the development of methodology for such research as they will be with the monitoring of efforts in the field. It is indeed unfortunate that it is so difficult to support this type of research; exploratory basic research is necessary to develop research designs and methods. Hypotheses can be stated with varying degrees of clarity but ways and means must be found to increase understanding of the community, mental-health concepts, the classification of psychiatric disorders, and so on. Many research projects are rejected just because they attempt to deal with these problems of definition, design, and methodology.

It is clear that these research efforts must go far beyond the field of psychiatry and its co-workers in psychology, social work, nursing, and occupational therapy; the development of meaningful, participating involvement of competent workers in other fields such as public health, sociology, anthropology and epidemiology will be essential.

Programmes for the prevention of psychiatric disorders and the promotion of mental health must be based on a recognition of the extent and nature of psychiatric disorders – an understanding not limited to diagnostic classification but including an awareness of the impingement of all human activities on mental health. To quote Dr. Henry Brill (1) ". . . there were mental health implications in all. . . . From allergy and aged to alcoholism, obesity and accidents, the trail led to such words as addiction, housing, then to poisoning, polio and pregnancy and finally ended with work accidents and workmen's compensation." Or as Lemkau says: "All prevention of disease prevents mental disease; all treatment of disease has as one aim the prevention of psychiatric complications of disease." (2)

We begin, in medicine, by symptomatic treatment. We hope to find a specific cause and apply specific treatment. If the cause is one which can be removed by environmental measures or by strengthening the host's resistance we can carry out primary prevention. For many years, psychiatrists have been enamoured of prevention and the lay movement may have been led to believe that mental illnesses can be prevented to an extent beyond our present capabilities.

In 1962, the American Public Health Association published *Mental Disorders: A Guide to Control Methods*. This publication follows the accepted ideas of "Control" and deals with prevention at three levels: primary, secondary and tertiary. Under the heading of primary prevention there are chapters entitled: "Mental Disorders of Known Etiology"; "Conditions of Unknown Etiology"; "Some General Measures for Prevention of Mental Disorders"; "Implications for Training of Administrators and other Specialists."

Insofar as "Mental Disorders of Known Etiology" are concerned, it is quite clear that primary prevention is not within the sphere of activity of the psychiatrist. Once the cause is known it becomes a matter of poison control, pre-natal care, control of infectious diseases, genetic counselling, dietary advice, and so on. These are traditional areas of public health concern; public health personnel and practicing physicians are prepared professionally for these activities, psychiatrists, in general, are not. Thus, practicing physicians and public health physicians or nurses should not feel uncomfortable in this area of primary prevention of mental disorders.

In more recent years, the work of Lemkau, Caplan, Pasamanick, Howell, MacLeod, and others, has done much to bring our efforts in the area of primary prevention to a focus. Lemkau's paper *"Prevention in Psychiatry"* (3) contains a number of statements which are worthy of repetition:

It appears to be the fate of psychiatrists that each time an illness once freely admitted as belonging in their bailiwicks yields up the secrets of its etiology, or even becomes subject to arrest by specific treatment, that disease is no longer considered psychiatric. . . . On the basis of scientific advances, the whole field of retardation has achieved a hopeful glow and it is proposed that it be transferred to another specialty – in part to paediatrics and in part to education. . . . Brings attention to the likelihood that behaviour disorders and psychiatric disorders are symptomatic, that all have a pathological base and that the triumphs of prevention (of psychiatric disorder) in syphilis, delirium, and phenylketonuric oliogophrenia may be duplicated in senility, schizophrenia, depressive illness and, perhaps, even the neuroses.

"Conditions of Unknown Etiology" are not yet in the area of primary control. They are, however, subject to control at the secondary and tertiary levels. Thus case-finding and follow-up should be of great concern for public health.

Under "Some General Measures for Prevention of Mental Disorders" we must consider the following: support in times of stress, prevention of maternal deprivation, improvement of child rearing practices, pre-natal care, reduction of radiological exposure, and genetic counselling. The development of adequate services in these areas should not be seen as a responsibility of mental-health services alone. Such programmes are concerned with total health and welfare of which psychiatric illness is just one aspect. The role of the mental-health professional in these areas is as a programme consultant or advisor.

The Social Breakdown Syndrome as postulated in Mental Disorders: A Guide to Control Methods is based on the concept that a capacity for development may be lost if social isolation is permitted during particular developmental periods. Social isolation or alienation is a break-down in communication. If we can keep people communicating (verbally, socially, emotionally, etc.) and if we help them through crisis situations, we should prevent many psychiatric conditions. Alienation or social isolation is a progressive and vicious circle – if we can impinge on the circle and break through the isolation much good will result.

Many approaches are being developed to deal with the problems of social isolation. These efforts include the establishment of counselling and guidance services, using both group and individual methods, related to support in times of stress, anticipation of significant life experiences, special social groupings and so on.

Dr. Alison I. Goldfarb, Chief of Geriatric Psychiatry at Mount Sinai Hospital, New York City, commenting on *Promoting Mental Health of Older People through Group Methods* (see Bibliography) states:

TABLE I*
SOME POISONS PRODUCING MENTAL DISORDERS

	Source									Types of Effect			
	Drugs	Animals	Food and Plants	Industrial	Malevolent Poisoning	Agricultural Chemicals	Addictive	In Consumers Goods and HH	Specific Antidote or Antagonist	Acute Symptoms	Toxic Psychoses	Perm. Brain Damage	Fatal
Abrin			FP		M					S			
Acetone	D			I				HH		S	P	BD	F
Acetylsalicylic Acid			FP							S		BD	F
Aconitine						Ag				S			F
Alkyl Mercury				I						S			
Aminophyllin	D								Barbiturates	S	P	BD	F
Amphetamine	D									S	P	BD	F
Aniline				I		Ag				S	P	BD	F
Arsenic	D				M			HH	BAL	S	P	?	F
BAL Dimercaprol	D									S			
Banthine	D								Stimulants	S	P	BD	F
Barbiturates	D									S	P		
Benadryl	D									S	P		
Benzol				I						S	P	?	F
Black Widow Spider		An							d-tubocurarine	S	P		
Bromides	D								i.v. NH₄CL	S	P		
Butazolidin	D								Antihistamines	S	P		
Cadmium				I						S	P		
Caffeine	D		FP				A?		Sedatives	S	P		
Camphor	D		FP	I						S	P		
Cannabinol			FP							S			
Carbon Disulphide				I						S	P	BD	F
Carbon Monoxide				I				HH		S	P	BD	F
Carbon Tetrachloride				I		Ag		HH	Ca. gluconate	S	P	BD	F
Cholinesterase Inhibitors	D			I					Atropine	S	P	BD	
Chlorothene				I						S			
Chlorothiazide	D									S	P		
Chlorpromazine	D								Methylphenidate	S	P	BD	
Cocaine	D						Ad			S	P		F
Colchicine	D								Atropine	S	P		F
Coniine			FP							S			

*Tables I–V are reprinted from *Mental Disorders: A Guide to Control Methods*, the American Public Health Association, 1962.

TABLE I (*continued*)

	Source									Types of Effect			
	Drugs	Animals	Food and Plants	Indus-trial	Malevolent Poisoning	Agri-cultural Chemicals	Addictive	In Consumers Goods and HH	Specific Antidote or Antagonist	Acute Symptoms	Toxic Psy-choses	Perm. Brain Damage	Fatal
Copper Salts	D			I		Ag							
Cyanides				I		Ag			Sodium Nitrite and Sodium Thiosulfate		P		F
Daphnin			FP					HH			P		F
DDT	D								Barbiturates	S	P		F
Digitalis	D		FP						Barbiturates	S	P		F
Dilantin									Potassium Cl.	S	P		
Ergot	D		FP						Caffeine	S	P		F
Ethanol	D						Ad		Barbiturates	S	P		
Ethylene Glycol Acetate				I					Na. acetate	S	P	BD	F
										S	P	BD	F
Germisol	D								Barbiturates	S			
Henbane	D								Paraldehyde	S			
Imipramine (Tofranil)	D								Barbiturates	S			
Iodine	D			I						S			
Iproniazid	D			I						S			
Iron	D			I						S			
Kerosene	D			I				HH	Analeptics	S	P		F
Lead				I				HH		S	P	BD	F
Lobeline			FP	I						S	P		
Lysergic Acid Diethylamide	D								Barbiturates	S	P		
Mercury	D			I					Dimercaprol	S	P		F
Mescaline	D		FP						Barbiturates	S	P	?	
Metaldehyde						Ag				S			
Methanol				I			Ad	HH	NaHCO₃	S	P	BD	F
Morphine	D		FP				Ad		Nalorphine	S	P	BD	F
Muscarine									Atropine	S	P		F
Naphthalene				I				HH		S			F
Parathion						Ag			O₂; atropine	S			F

TABLE I (*concluded*)

	Source									Types of Effect			
	Drugs	Animals	Food and Plants	Indus-trial	Malevolent Poisoning	Agri-cultural Chemicals	Addictive	In Consumers Goods and HH	Specific Antidote or Antagonist	Acute Symptoms	Toxic Psy-choses	Perm. Brain Damage	Fatal
Phenacetin (Acetophenetidin)	D									S	P		
Phenergan	D								Paraldehyde	S	P		F
Phenmetrazine	D									S			
Phenol				I				HH		S	P		
Phenylbutazone	D								Antihistamines	S	P		
Phosphorus (yellow)	D			I				HH		S	P		F
Pyrethrum				I		Ag		HH		S	P		
Quinacrine (Atabrine)	D									S	P		
Rauwolfia	D		FP						Atropine	S	P		
Ricin	D		FP	I						S	P		F
Saccharine				I				HH		S	P		
Scorpions		An							Serum; Barbiturates	S	P		
Snake Venoms		An							Noradrenalin antivenins	S	P		
Sodium Hypochlorite	D			I				HH		S	P		F
Solanin			FP					HH		S	P	Potatoes eaten by children	F
Squill	D	An								S	P		
Strammonium	D		FP						Barbiturates	S	P		
Strychnine	D				M				O$_2$; barbiturates	S	P		F
Sympathomimetic Amines	D						A			S	P		
Thallium	D					Ag		HH	BAL	S	P	BD	
Thiocyanates	D			I				HH		S	P		
Toluene				I						S			
Tricreylphosphate				I				HH		S	P		
Turpentine				I						S	P		
Vanadium					M					S			F

TABLE II
INFECTIONS PRODUCING MENTAL DISORDERS

	Agent*	Reservoir	Vector	Personal Contact	Effective Immunization Active/Passive	Effective Rx to Prevent Brain Damage	Occurrence	Acute Symptoms	Permanent Brain Damage Fetal	Permanent Brain Damage Childhood	Permanent Brain Damage Adult	Notes
Aseptic meningitis												
Group B Coxsackie	V	Man		PC	No	No	Common	Ac				
Chicken pox	V	Man		PC	No	No	Universal	Ac		Ch		
Smallpox	V	Man		PC	Yes		Not in USA	Ac				
Encephalitides	V	Birds?	Mosquitoes	No	No See Text	No		Ac		Ch	Ad	
Eastern encephalitis	V	Wild birds	Mosquitoes	No	No	No	Sporadic or Epidemic	Ac		Ch		
Western encephalitis	V	Wild birds	Mosquitoes	No	No	No	Sporadic or Epidemic					
St. Louis encephalitis	V	Wild birds	Mosquitoes	No	No	No	Sporadic or Epidemic	Ac		Ch		
Pertussis	B	Man		PC	Active		Common	Ac		Ch	Ad	
Encephalitis lethargica					No	No	Epidemic	Ac		Ch	Ad	Apparently has disappeared from the world.
Influenza	V	Man		PC	Active	No	Epidemic	Ac	No	Ch	Ad	
Measles	V	Man		PC	Passive-gamma globulin	No	Universal	Ac		Ch	0.02%	

*V = virus; B = Bacterium or bacillus; Sp = Spirochete; Prot = Protozoon; ? = suspected; blanks = not known; F = fetal.

TABLE II (concluded)

	Agent*	Reservoir	Vector	Personal Contact	Effective Immunization Active/Passive	Effective Rx to Prevent Brain Damage	Occurrence	Acute Symptoms	Permanent Brain Damage			Notes
									Fetal	Childhood	Adult	
Meningococcus meningitis	V	Man		PC	None	Sulfas and antibiotics	Sporadic and Epidemic	Ac		Ch	Ad	Especially dangerous in infants. Mental deficiency.
Mononucleosis	Unkn.	Man?		PC?	None	None	Common	1% children		Ch		
Mumps	V	Man		PC	Active; lasts two years	None	Universal	Ac	?	Ch?	?	
Pneumococcal pneumonia	B	Man		PC	None	Sulfas and antibiotics	Common	Ac				
Rheumatic fever	?	Man		PC	None		Frequent	Ac	?	Ch?	?	Is a complication of streptococcal disease.
Rubella	V	Man		PC	Passive-gamma globulin	None	Universal		F			About 10% of fetal infections in first trimester result in anomalies.
Syphilis	Sp.	Man		PC	None	Penicillin	Frequent		F	Ch	Ad	
Toxoplasmosis	Prot.	Many mammals		Congenital	None	Sulfonamides?	Scattered		F?			
Tuberculosis	B	Man		PC	Active	Isoniazid	Scattered			Ch	Ad	

*V = virus; B = Bacterium or Bacillus; Sp = Spirochete; Prot. = Protozoon; ? = suspected; blanks = not known; F = fetal.

TABLE III
SOME GENETIC DISEASES WHICH MAY PRODUCE MENTAL DISORDERS

	Mendelian R = recessive D = dominant	Age of Manifestation	Treatment	Carrier Identification	Approx. Frequency	Lab. Diagnosis	Proportion of Cases Due to Mutations
Cerebral lipidoses	R	Various	None	Some types	1:25,000	No	Negligible
Galactosemia	R	Infant	Dietary	Yes	Unknown	Yes	Negligible
Phenylketonuria	R	Infant	Dietary	Yes	1:20,000	Yes	Negligible
Gargoylism	R	Infant	None	No	<1:25,000	Yes	Negligible
Gargoylism (sex-linked)	R	Child	None	No	<1:50,000	Yes	Approx. $\frac{1}{3}$
Acrocephalosyndactyly	D	Congenital	None	Yes	Unknown	No	Most
Ocular hypertelorism	D	Congenital	None	Yes	Unknown	No	Unknown
Huntington's chorea	D	Late adult	None	No	1:25,000	No	Approx. $\frac{1}{3}$
Tuberous sclerosis	D	Variable	None	Yes	1:30,000	No	Approx. $\frac{1}{4}$

TABLE IV
NUTRITIONAL DEFICIENCIES WHICH PRODUCE MENTAL DISORDERS

Name	Deficiency Foods	Acute Brain Syndrome	Chronic Brain Syndrome	Mental Retardation	Notes
Beriberi	Thiamine	S			
Kwashiorkor	Multiple, especially protein	S	Chr	MR	Anorexia in weaning infants
Pellagra	Niacin	S	Chr	?	
Wernicke's encephalopathy	Thiamine	S	Chr		Especially in chronic alcoholics
Anoxemia	Oxygen	S	Chr	MR	

S = Acute brain syndrome.
Chr = Chronic brain syndrome.
MR = Mental retardation as a residual.

TABLE V
MENTAL DISORDERS CAUSED BY GENERAL SYSTEMIC DISEASES

	Brain Syndromes		Prevention	Corr. Rx	Effective Maintenance Rx
	Acute	Chronic			
Addison's disease Adrenocortical deficiency	Ac	Chr	No	No	Corticosteroids
Pernicious anemia Inability to absorb Vitamin B12 due to absence of "intrinsic" gastric enzyme	Ac		No	No	Liver
Cushing's syndrome Hypercortisone	Ac			Operate if due to basophilic adenoma	
Erythroblastosis fetalis Maternal antibodies destroy fetal blood cells		Chr	Rh typing	Exchange transfusion	No
Hyperbilirubinemia Liver defect			No	Exchange transfusion	
Hyperthyroidism	Ac		No	Operative	Yes
Cretinism Hypothyroidism	Ac	Chr	Iodine in salt?	No	Yes
Diabetes Hyperinsulinism	Ac	Chr	No	No	Insulin
Intracranial masses	Ac	Chr	No	Surgery or antibiotics	No
Arteriosclerosis	Ac	Chr	No	No	No
Senile deterioration	Ac	Chr	No	No	No
Mongolism		Chr	No	No	No

What shines through is that older persons bring practical problems to the leader, that they focus their attention upon him and that they benefit from the opportunity to bring things to him and from his attitude toward them. . . . Because it favors the development of a relationship which the older person may otherwise be disinclined to accept or may be unable to find, the group may prove to be a practical . . . as well as less expensive . . . way of providing what many aged persons need if they are to learn, relearn, or release their capacities for adjustment to a community which tends to pose them diffiicult problems as their ability decreases.

A further example of this type of activity is provided by "The Well-Being Clinics" developed by Dr. Allister MacLeod and Mrs. Phyllis Poland in conjunction with the YWCA in Montreal. The results of group discussions as used in the Crestwood Heights project in Toronto provide further evidence of the efficacy of such methods in providing opportunities for the emotional development of school children.

The chapter entitled "Implications for the Training of Administrators and Other Specialists" is well worth reading. It is apparent that all of us in our different specialities require more knowledge of each others' roles and of how our activities can augment or minimize each others' efforts. While recent developments have been encouraging, it is also true that some of the major changes which appear to be desirable, particularly in respect of preventive activities and the provision of patient care, are being impeded and delayed by many existing attitudes towards mental illness and the mentally ill. It would appear that much more will have to be done to change the attitudes of those responsible for major legislation and administration. It seems apparent that the public at large and many community groups are ahead of the professions and governmental authorities in their attitude towards mental illness and in their desire to see improvements in the services provided. We must find ways of mobilizing this general public support and using it to bring about necessary changes.

The work of Dr. Alexander Leighton and his associates seems destined to make major contributions to our understanding of communities and the development of mental illness therein. While biology, heredity, current circumstances, life experiences, and so on may all play a part in the etiology of psychiatric and psychological disorders in an individual, Leighton appears to accept that psycho-neurotic patterns are primarily derived from life experiences with varying degrees of hereditary and physiological predisposition; personality disorders are conceived of as being basically "constitutional," that is, whatever the cause, the condition arises early, pervades the personality and remains relatively fixed throughout life; and that heredity is a major factor in both schizophrenia and the affective psychoses. Thereafter, it appears that the socio-cultural environment can influence the development or prevention of disorders. These sociocultural conditions may well have selective influences on the appearance and persistence of malfunctioning which may lead to psychiatric disorders. Social disintegration – not just a moving away from functional effectiveness but including a relative lack of patterning in the system may be incited by: a high frequency of broken homes; few and weak associations; few and weak leaders; few patterns of recreation; high frequency of hostility; high frequency of crime and delinquency; weak and fragmented communication.

Communities, according to Leighton, are apt to become disintegrated as a result of: recent disasters; widespread ill health; extensive poverty; cultural confusion; widespread secularization; extensive migration; rapid, widespread social change. Community social disintegration results in psychological stress, lack of resources for dealing with stress, and, thereafter, psychiatric disorders.

Leighton and his co-workers pose a number of hypotheses which are then examined in the light of the data gathered in their community studies. (4)

1. "Socio-cultural disintegration leads to physical insecurity and then to psychiatric disorder." Their findings indicate that individuals living in depressed areas have a high risk of psychiatric disorder regardless of their own position of economic advantage and conclude that psychiatric illness is not the result of physical insecurity.

2. "Socio-cultural disintegration fosters mental health by the degree to which it permits freedom of sexual expression." They found that the highest prevalence of psychosomatic symptoms were present in those with the least sexual restraint. They do not refute this hypothesis but raise doubts as to its validity.

3. "Socio-cultural disintegration fosters mental health by the degree to which it permits freedom of hostile and aggressive expression." Their evidence indicates that groups in which aggression and hostility are freely expressed have the greatest prevalence of symptoms.

4. "Socio-cultural disorder fosters psychiatric disorders because of the limitations put on the giving and receiving of love." Their evidence supports this: great numbers of broken homes, separation of parents, membership in few associations, overt hostility in the groups, and poor communication.

5. "Social disintegration fosters psychiatric disorders by interfering with the achievement of socially valued ends by legitimate means." Their evidence supports this hypothesis.

6. "Socio-cultural disintegration fosters psychiatric disorders by interfering with spontaneity." The evidence suggests that while people can get away with more things in a disintegrated area, the choice of things one might like to do is very limited. The integrated communities appear to offer a wider range of opportunities.

7. "Social disintegration fosters psychiatric disorders by interfering with a person's orientation regarding his place in society and sense of membership in human groups." This is supported by the evidence that people in depressed areas feel mentally and morally inferior.

8. "Social disintegration fosters psychiatric disorder by interfering with the individual's sense of membership in a moral order." Their evidence suggests that cultural confusion, secularization, lack of membership in associations, lack of leaders, poor communication, all contribute to high incidence of psychiatric disorders and, conversely, that the moral order of a community has a regulative power in terms of mental health.

Paul Lemkau, at a recent meeting of the World Federation for Mental Health, reviewed the activities of public-health and mental-health workers and demonstrated how the common concern about morbidity and disablement is bringing together the efforts of many people. He indicated his belief that we in psychiatry may not be fully aware of how much prevention has taken place and that we appear to be moving on to firmer ground in respect of certain disorders at least. While recognizing the multi-factorial nature of certain mental disorders, such as senility and arteriosclerosis, he stressed our knowledge of the "Social Breakdown Syndrome" and social deprivation of children and their potential importance in primary prevention.

While specific preventive measures are not yet available for certain illnesses, such as schizophrenia, it would seem that a recognition of the contributions of Crestwood Heights and Stirling County, the concept of the social breakdown syndrome, and social deprivation in childhood, provide us with reasonably firm ground on which to base a social programme for the improvement of mental health and the prevention of at least some psychiatric illnesses.

At this time it is necessary, in the broadest terms, to consider the importance of social action in the promotion of mental health and the prevention of mental ill-health. On the basis of research findings, it would seem reasonable to suggest that such social action should have the following objectives:

1. The avoidance of socio-cultural disintegration;
2. The maintenance of group standards of behaviour;

3. The elimination of exploitation of personal, racial, religious, cultural, and other differences for economic, political or other reasons as there is an indication that groups in which hostility and aggression are freely expressed have the highest prevalence of symptoms;

4. The creation of social programmes to promote the integrity of the family, group activities, and of other community developments to support the individual and his family;

5. The establishment of socially valuable objectives as goals for our society and recognition of the contributions of individuals to the achievement of these goals;

6. The development of programmes to clarify and ensure the place of the individual in our society;

7. The enrichment of the environment of children in all socio-economic-educational groups to permit the maximum development of their individual potential.

When our present social and psychiatric problems are viewed in the light of these principles, we may well have reason for concern. It would not appear unreasonable to suggest that our society is becoming increasingly hedonistic – the individual must have immediate gratification or satisfaction of needs regardless of the social cost, or, in the long term, the cost to the individual concerned. Too commonly, one hears expression of concern about one's place in society, of disillusionment regarding one's contribution to society, and of isolation and loneliness. This hedonistic standard is now affecting all our social structures; social structures and sanctions on behaviour have always existed for the good of society as a whole even though it has been recognized that individuals might well suffer personally in order to preserve society as a whole. While it is true that Freud postulated the psychological scheme that demonstrates the diffiiculties which repression and other psychological defence mechanisms cause for the individual, he always recognized that these were socially necessary and that sublimation of the individual's drives or instincts through socially acceptable activities might well be essential in the development and maintenance of a reasonable society. It would appear that all social groups have need for acceptable group objectives with which the individual can identify and from which he can gain personal satisfaction and a sense of social value which justify to him his continuing contributions to society and the deferment of gratification of some of his intense innate needs.

Dr. J. Aufreiter has expressed a point of view on the dynamics of many of the conditions we see in psychiatry which, for me, adds further clarification to these points. According to Dr. Aufreiter, all individuals have basic needs for which they seek gratification. If gratification is not forthcoming, then anger and aggression develop followed by feelings of guilt. This guilt is dealt with either by depression which is directed inwards or by paranoia which is directed outwards. These reactions are accompanied or followed by efforts at reparation. It is important to realize that immediate and selfish satisfaction of these basic drives can lead to the same processes. We must, therefore, conclude that gratification must be obtained through constructive social activities (a euphemism for work) which will lead to acceptable satisfaction of these basic drives or wishes. While there may be immediate and temporary relief following the expression of aggression or the satisfaction of sexual drives, it is clear that the individual will not make a satisfactory long-term adjustment unless there is a concurrent satisfactory level of personal and social acceptance. Demonstration of such ways of dealing with the individual's instinctual drives is perhaps the most critical task of a parent or parent substitute and it would appear that adults who as children did not assimilate this way of behaviour may well have mental-health problems.

There are many interesting contradictions in the mental-health field. In psychoanalysis and in psychotherapy, there is frequent reference to the maintenance of a level of frustration in which gratification of many of the patient's demands is avoided. Many, but by no means all, therapists insist that patients will not make progress unless they themselves pay for their therapy. In this scheme of things, the patient's ego should be consistently strengthened so as to provide an acceptable state of balance between the internal drives, the internal restrictions on behaviour, and the real world in which the patient lives. The patient must pay or must give up something (that is, make a choice regarding the time when a particular drive is to be satisfied) in order to feel justified in taking "treatment" from the therapist. By contrast, it is interesting to observe the number of people in the area of social action who advocate gratification of impulses without requiring effective social participation – this appears to be so in the field of industrial relations, education, family life, and so on. As Leighton observed in his comments on freedom of sexual expression, these ideas are usually more popular with social scientists than with mental-health professionals, although they would appear to be gaining an increasing number of adherents in the mental-health field as well. It is quite possible that the efforts of those working in the field of pathology to extend into areas of prevention are based on the experience of what happens to "sick" individuals rather than to those members of our society who maintain an acceptable level of social function. It is clear that specific programmes for treatment must be based on more information about total rather than abnormal populations. As an example of this we have a recent study of college students in the United States. In this study college students were asked to pick their most mentally healthy classmates. The resulting group of students was found to have a significantly higher proportion of serious conflicts with parents (in many cases, the students had left home because of this) than did a random sample of other students. If they had been sick students instead of the most healthy, we could probably have attributed their illness to "conflict with authority."

All experiences to date would indicate that our society must provide opportunities for individual development, for individual satisfaction, for a sense of individual worth and social recognition and participation if we are to look forward to better mental health in the future.

It would be easy to avoid mention of political systems and national policies when discussing primary prevention in the mental health field. It would, however, be unrealistic to do so. For too many years we have concerned ourselves with individual action in the mental health field. As indicated earlier, we must now, of necessity, enter the arena of social action.

Transcultural psychiatry has not yet clarified the effects of different cultures on mental health. We in the Western world pride ourselves on our physical accomplishments, we are proud of our individual freedom, and of our social-welfare programmes. There is, however, a quality to all of these. Are they developed as part of a social-action programme or are they political expedients? The British National Health Service, based on a social philosophy expressed in the Beveridge Report, while beset with problems, has indeed made great contributions to the health of the British people. At the end of the second world war, Canada was filled with a spirit of optimism: we had had our reconstruction reports, all Canadians were to have a great future, no one was to suffer from want; universal old age pensions, unemployment insurance, family allowances, and the National Health Grants Programme were to be the foundation on which our future would be built. Unfortunately, no provisions were made whereby these programmes would automatically adjust to changing conditions, thus, while the value of these programmes has been evident, they have frequently been eroded by change in external, social factors, and have only with great reluctance, often with an eye to elections, been amended. How can older citizens, less privileged families with young children, widows, and other dependent members of our society, feel

that they have a recognized place in our communities when subjected
to this kind of treatment? Why would they not feel lost, unwanted, and
without a valued place in our society? Is it any wonder that they become
cynical, socially isolated, and suffer from various psychosomatic and
psychiatric difficulties? This is equally true of our young children, our
adolescents, and our handicapped. Services are too grudgingly given,
often as a special concession rather than as a right of a free citizen in
a free society which is proud of its accomplishments and which recognizes the individual's essential dignity. There is, however, reason for
hope; in the United States there are such good examples as the Peace
Corps, the messages on mental health and retardation, and sweeping
changes in social welfare philosophy, not to mention the concept of the
Great Society. In Canada, we have cuso, the Company of Young
Canadians, ARDA, and the Canada Welfare Plan. If only these could
be mobilized to give every Canadian a feeling of participation in a
valued and valuable programme; were an attachment to such ideals to
be engendered, it would seem that many of the problems faced by each
of us and our society as a whole would be reduced.

The rationalization of our federal, provincial, and municipal systems
is essential if we are to assure to everyone the housing, educational,
counselling, recreational, social welfare, and health programmes which
are essential if we are to have a truly preventive programme, in the
primary sense, in our country. No one must be denied the essential
opportunity of personal and social fulfilment because of some argument
over jurisdiction; in times of war these difficulties can be overcome,
surely they can be overcome in times of peace. Nor should services
necessary for personal and social fulfilment be denied on the basis of
cost: society can afford that which is necessary. And just as highways
are only as good as their users, great physical monuments, subways, air-
ports, and so on, can be symbols of the aims, objectives, and value
systems of a society and are often essential to physical comfort, but
they may remain as monuments to our social failures unless concur-
rently necessary opportunities are provided for the individual members
of our society to find a satisfying and accepted place. Morbidity has
been reduced, life expectancy has increased markedly, society must
now provide opportunities for effective, satisfying "living" for those
whose physical health has been improved and whose lives have been
lengthened. There is reason for optimism.

It now appears reasonable to assume that the provision of effective
counselling services – for marriage, for parenthood, for children, for
adolescents, for the handicapped, for the unemployed, for the aged –

could do much to avoid the social-breakdown syndrome, deprivation in childhood, and isolation, and thus materially improve the mental health of our people.

There are a number of special areas which require further consideration. As indicated earlier, child guidance clinics have been available for a number of decades and frequently one hears comments regarding their value. In this connection, I refer to a review entitled "Continuity and Intervention in Emotional Disturbance" by W. W. Lewis, which reads in part:

The treatment procedures used in child guidance clinics are based implicitly on two hypotheses . . . the continuity hypothesis, that emotional disturbance in a child is symptomatic of a continuing psychological process that may lead to an adult mental illness . . . the intervention hypothesis, therapeutic intervention enhances the child's present adjustment and reduces the likelihood that he will experience serious mental problems in later life.

Lewis states his conclusions on the continuity and intervention hypotheses as follows:

Two working hypotheses in clinical treatment of disturbed children have been examined in this review. The continuity hypothesis, that emotionally disturbed children will become mentally ill adults, has received only mild support. If one begins with mental patients and reviews their developmental history, he is likely to find a record of childhood problems. If one begins with a population of children identified as emotionally disturbed and follows the whole group to adulthood, the evidence is mixed. Neither of the two large scale followup studies was designed specifically to test the continuity hypothesis, so the conclusion must be guarded. The conclusion of the Dallas study is that it is hazardous to predict particular forms of adult mental illness from childhood symptoms, at least in the language we customarily use to talk about children's problems. In any event, only a small proportion of the total group of children became so disturbed as adults that they had to be admitted to a mental hospital. The St. Louis study, on the other hand, identified psychiatric problems in almost two-thirds of its former child patients but very few of the problems identified could be called serious or incapacitating, and, as in the Dallas study, no accurate predictions could have been made on the basis of presenting symptoms in childhood. So far as the continuity hypothesis is concerned, we must at least conclude that it is incomplete. The extent to which a childhood predisposition to mental illness influences appearance of problems in adult life is not entirely clear but it is apparently not a determining factor. In this perspective, Levitt's suggestion that time may be more important than treatment has more meaning. That some disturbed children will grow up to be disturbed adults is undoubtedly true, but many others will grow up to be ordinary adults with no more than their share of problems.

The second hypothesis of clinical treatment, that therapeutic intervention enhances the general adjustment status of disturbed children, has received even less support than the continuity hypothesis. The regularity with which the two-thirds to three-fourths improvement figure occurs in studies of disturbed children, regardless of treatment, suggests a widely shared bias that allows us to see all but the most obstreperous children as "better than they were."

The most convincing evidence for the effectiveness of intervention is in studies using criteria more specific than assessment of general adjustment. While some might argue that sociometric scores, questionnaires, and tests beg the real question of whether the child is better, the fact is that as outcome variables they reflect differential change while global judgments of improvement do not. One way of interpreting this difference, of course, is that as research tools, judgments about general adjustment are simply not as reliable as test scores or ratings on specific items of behaviour. However, in the absence of compelling confirmation of the continuity hypothesis, we may need to re-examine what we hope to accomplish by intervention rather than concluding that the evaluation of intervention is a hopeless undertaking. If we do not postulate a linear relationship between emotional disturbance in childhood and mental illness in adulthood, the treatment of symptoms may be all we can realistically undertake. If we cannot aspire to reconstruction of personality that will have long range beneficial effects, we can modify disturbing behaviour in specific ways in present social contexts. This more modest aspiration may not only be more realistic, but it may be all that is required of the child-helping professions in a society that is relatively open and provides a variety of opportunity systems in which a child can reconcile his personal needs with society's expectations of him. (5)

This review is strongly recommended as a reference source for anyone interested in the development of children's services.

There are a number of conditions which may be collectively referred to as psycho-social: alcoholism, drug addiction, suicide, behaviour disorders and delinquency, and much of the symptomatology seen in geriatric psychoses. The more we study these conditions the more we realize that they result from the failure of our present social patterns to meet adequately the needs of many individuals. Thus, to ask the question "can we prevent alcoholism or drug addiction?" is to ask whether it is possible to prevent the many psycho-social ills which confront us today.

This failure of our social patterns to provide for the individual needs of our people is the basis of many of today's psycho-social ills. The child who becomes delinquent is often seeking an outlet for himself which will make him stand out in his group, which will give him a feeling of importance and through this an inner satisfaction. The aging person who becomes a problem usually feels abandoned, and, in fact, often is. To him, life no longer seems to have meaning and he feels himself to be a burden to his relatives rather than a contributing member of his family or social group. The drug addict is similarly seeking escape from unpleasant realities which are often based on the feeling of not being wanted or of not belonging to a group. He frequently seeks escape through association with other individuals in an environment which accepts him without question and it is here that his addiction is usually developed.

The prevention of psycho-social illness, of which drug addiction is an example, presents one of the major problems of our day. There is, to my knowledge, no evidence that the increased availability of alcohol, LSD, marijuana, and other drugs, or the recognition of addictions as being illnesses, has contributed to a reduction in the extent and nature of these problems. There is evidence in Great Britain that the restriction of alcohol during the second world war may have reduced alcoholism and, to quote Professor Carstairs (6), "the reduction in severe alcoholism in this country [Great Britain] can confidently be ascribed to taxation which has made it too expensive to drink really heavily. Similarly, legal sanctions have cut down the amount of drug addiction." It would seem reasonable to assume that the incidence of these conditions is increasing as the addicting agents become more widely available and as the social sanctions against such conditions are reduced. The philosophy of increased availability, maintenance of addiction, and the lowering of social sanctions may well be nihilistic, as these tend to support pathology rather than health. The prevention of these conditions is a challenge which can be met if you and I together with the other citizens who constitute our communities are prepared to make the necessary efforts.

In doing this, the first essential is that the homes in which our children are brought up should provide for their full needs. Naturally this includes the necessities of life: proper diet, proper clothing, warmth, and comfort, but, more important, it also means love and security; the infant must feel wanted. One wonders how such a climate can be provided in the over-crowded slums of our cities, in homes where there is discord between parents, in homes torn by alcoholism, separation, or divorce, or when other factors are present to mar the environment of the growing child.

The second need is for a re-evaluation of our moral and ethical standards. To develop normally, a child must grow in a proper atmosphere of right and wrong, or good and bad. From the first he must learn that certain actions on his part are to his advantage while others bring undesired results; that his behaviour in a group is necessarily related to that of others in the group and, if he wants to get along, he has to give as well as receive benefits. As adults we must realize our responsibility to older people and recognize the contribution they have already made to our society and to us individually. Today, too many older people are living in very small rooms, too many are in municipal homes, and far too many are entering mental hospitals. No one would ever advocate that a mentally disturbed old person should be elsewhere than in a mental hospital, but too many older people are deteriorating mentally because they are made to feel unwanted and have no further useful part to play.

In meeting the challenge of all of the psycho-social conditions, the clergy has a vital role. No other group in our society has the same access to the individual; through this relationship many of the social and moral standards of our communities and of the people who make up these communities can be prescribed.

Similarly, the school plays a leading part in the provision of better psycho-social conditions. The role of the school is to teach and this includes teaching for future living. The school and, perhaps in a more personal and meaningful way, the teachers have a terrific impact on the growing child. The attitudes, behaviour, and moral values of the teacher often set the behaviour pattern for our children and this is particularly true of children coming from discordant homes. In addition to these general effects, the school has a more specific contribution. During the early school years children are more likely to show their first difficulties in adjusting to social situations. These may be seen in a variety of patterns but, in all cases of deviate behaviour, the child needs adequate assessment, guidance, and help, so that he may learn proper methods of adjustment.

The community, through such organizations as church groups, youth centres, Boy Scouts and Girl Guides, has an essential role in helping teenagers and young adults through this rather difficult period of growing up. Community programmes must aim to meet the needs of the growing child through the development of healthful and health-giving activities. The basic need at this period is the satisfaction which comes from being a useful member of the group. Children want to conform and yet they want the freedom of adults even before they have sufficiently matured to handle perplexing social situations. These programmes must allow scope for individual initiative and group activity and, through proper guidance and organization, must help the very young and the teenagers to adjust and handle these situations. Recreation and group activities for teenagers and young adults ought not to be based on the negative idea of keeping them off the streets and away from undesirable hangouts, even though these may be worthy objectives. Nor should they be intended to replace family activities or to make life easier for the parents. Rather, they should be provided to meet the needs of the teen-ager and young adult so that they will develop through wholesome activities into healthy, satisfied, and useful members of our adult society.

What positive steps can be advocated to achieve adequate development from infancy to maturity? When the home is broken, a child should be placed in a foster home or in other circumstances where parent substitutes and the love and kindness so necessary for him can, as far as possible, be provided. Is it too much to hope that our prosperous society could provide adequate, useful, and individually satisfying activities for older people who are threatened with frustration and abandonment? When social and moral standards are threatened, should not the churches and other community organizations assume the initiative in exercising an increasing influence in all our communities which are underprivileged, whether physically, morally, or socially, to organize these areas in such a way that their residents can gain motivations which will enable them to go forward together towards self-improvement and the improvement of the community around them? It is not suggested that schools should replace the home in providing the essential background for the growing child but rather that, receiving pliable children, they may beneficially influence the further development of their personalities. Home and school must work together to develop children who can become happy and useful members of our free society. Attitudes towards civic affairs, towards drugs, and other depressing influences are subtle. They are seldom successfully taught in an intellectual way; rather, the young child absorbs attitudes from his total environment. Early help is essential if he is to achieve adequate adjustment in the future. Within a few years, patterns of behaviour are established which will be very difficult to overcome even by individual therapy. Most of our social deviates – delinquents, addicts, and neurotics – have a background of poor adjustment during this period and we know too well how difficult it is to alter these behaviour patterns in later life.

In addition to adequate preparation of our youth for future life, we must remove the slums and undesirable hangouts from our communities and provide proper accommodation, healthy environments, and, more important, individually satisfying activities for those who live in these areas. In community planning, let us ever be conscious of the inner needs of our people – conscious that these are in many ways more important than their physical needs which today we are striving to fulfil. The sum total of these activities would represent the basis for the community effort.

I have chosen to concentrate on general measures in the area of social action rather than on those specific items covered in the third chapter of the A.P.H.A. Manual which I discussed earlier, as I believe, on the basis of our present knowledge, that general social measures, which are capable of achievement, could do much more for the mental health of a population than can the limited number of specific preventive actions now available to us – even though each of these must be individually applied as they become known to us.

The question "Who is to prevent mental illness?" is frequently asked. Obviously, we all have a responsibility in this area: the physician (regardless of his speciality or area of work) in respect of medical action, all of the helping professions in respect of social and psychological opportunities for development, and the total community, particularly its leaders, in respect of social action. In this connection, the institutionalization of responsibility gives cause for concern; as our communities become larger, as family relationships change, and as tax-supported programmes replace individual responsibility, there may be a continuing shift of total responsibility to impersonal institutions. This situation would be the antithesis of good mental health which is a state in which the individual feels accepted, worthwhile, and contributing, and is able to gain satisfaction from his meaningful, responsible activities as an individual, as a member of a family, and as one of the individuals in the larger social groups which make up our communities.

Lemkau summarizes the present position as follows (2):

First: every model of pathological process produces diseases that have psychiatric symptoms. Preventive psychiatry is an inevitable component of all diseases prevention and every physician has a role as preventor of psychiatric illnesses. Regardless of how narrow his concept of his speciality, he cannot avoid this role. Second: Social deprivation, emotional conflict and environmental stress are included as models of processes which produce pathological behaviour. The first of these, because of successful research in the last two decades, has begun to have increased specificity while the other two remain too much for anyone's satisfaction as influences of a general type leading to various types of ill health. Each of the three offers opportunities for direct preventive action; however, because of their non-specific character and probably because of time relationships, the evaluation of preventive effect is extremely difficult. Nevertheless, it can be said that the concept of preventive psychiatry is a little less vague and tenuous than it was a decade ago. The theory is tighter and the opportunity for action is more inviting.

REFERENCES

1. HILLEBOE, H. G. and G. W. LARIMORE. (Eds.). *Preventive Medicine* (2nd ed.). Philadelphia: W. B. Saunders, 1965.
2. LEMKAU, P. V. Prospects for the prevention of mental illnesses. *Ment. Hyg.*, 1966, 50:172–79.

3. LEMKAU, P. V. Prevention in psychiatry. *Amer. J. publ. Hlth*, 1965, 55: 554–60.
4. LEIGHTON, D., J. S. HARDING, D. B. MACKLIN, A. LEIGHTON, and A. D. MACMILLAN. *The Character of Danger: Psychiatric Symptoms in Selected Communities.* New York: Basic Books, 1963.
5. LEWIS, W. W. Continuity and intervention in emotional disturbance: A review. *Exceptional Children*, 1965, 31:465–75.
6. CARSTAIRS, G. M. Preventive psychiatry: Is there such a thing? *J. ment. Sci.*, 1958, 104:63–71.
7. HUGHES, C. C., M. A. TREMBLAY, R. N. RAPOPORT, and A. LEIGHTON. *People of Cove and Woodlot.* New York: Basic Books, 1960.
8. LEIGHTON, A. *My Name is Legion.* New York: Basic Books, 1959.

BIBLIOGRAPHY

AMERICAN PUBLIC HEALTH ASSOCIATION, Program Area Committee on Mental Health. *Mental Disorders: A Guide to Control Methods.* New York: American Public Health Association, September 1962.

ANDERSON, U. M. and R. M. BANNERMAN. The future role of the health department in medical genetics. *Amer. J. publ. Hlth,* 1965, 55:866–71.

ARIETI, SYLVANO (ed.). *American Handbook of Psychiatry,* vols. 1, 2, 3. New York: Basic Books, 1959 and 1966.

BELKIN, M., E. A. SUCHMAN, B. LEVINSON, and H. JACOBZINER. Mental health training program for the Child Care Conference. *Amer. J. publ. Hlth,* 1965, 55:1046–56.

BELLAK, L. (ed.). *Handbook of Community Psychiatry and Community Mental Health.* New York: Grune & Stratton, 1964.

BENDER, L. Psychopathic behaviour disorders in children. In R. M. LINDNER and R. V. SELIGER (eds.). *Handbook of Correctional Psychology.* New York: Philosophical Library, 1947. Pp. 360–77.

BERGEN, B. J. Professional communities and the evaluation of demonstration projects in community mental health. *Amer. J. publ. Hlth,* 1965, 55:1057–66.

BOWLBY, J. *Maternal Care and Mental Health.* World Health Organization, Monograph Series no. 2. Geneva: World Health Organization, 1952.

BRIM, O. G., JR. *Education for Child Rearing.* New York: Russell Sage Foundation, 1959.

BRUHN, J. G., E. N. BRANDT, and M. SHACKLEFORD. Incidence of treated mental illness in three Pennsylvania communities. *Amer. J. publ. Hlth,* 1966, 56:871–83.

CAPLAN, GERALD. (Ed.). *Prevention of Mental Disorders in Children: Initial Explorations.* New York: Basic Books, 1961.

—— *Principles of Preventive Psychiatry.* New York: Basic Books, 1964.

COLEMAN, J. V., S. T. CLAUDEWELL, and B. J. BERGEN. A teaching program in public health psychiatry. *Amer. J. Psychiat.,* 1965, 122:285–88

COLLARD, E. J. The Public health nurse in aftercare programs for the mentally ill: the present status. *Amer. J. publ. Hlth,* 1966, 56:210–17.

CRAVENS, RICHARD B. "Impact of Recent Federal Legislation: Community Mental Health Services." Presented at the American Public Health Association Annual Meeting, 3 November, 1966.

CROCETTI, G. M. and P. V. LEMKAU. Public opinion of psychiatric home care in an urban area. *Amer. J. publ. Hlth,* 1963, 53:409–17.

CUMMING, J. and E. CUMMING. *Ego and Milieu: Theory and Practice of Environmental Therapy.* New York: Atherton Press, 1962.

EATON, J. W. and R. J. WEIL. *Culture and Mental Disorders: A Comparative Study of the Hutterites and Other Populations.* Glencoe: Free Press, 1955.

EISENBERG, L. Preventive psychiatry: if not now, when? In HENRY P. DAVID, (Ed.). *International Trends in Mental Health.* New York: McGraw-Hill, 1966. Pp. 63 ff.

—— and E. M. GRUENBERG. The current status of secondary prevention in child psychiatry. *Amer. J. Orthopsychiat.*, 1961, 31:355–67.

—— The strategic deployment of the child psychiatrist in preventive psychiatry. *J. child Psychol. Psychiat.*, 1961, 2:229–41.

—— Preventive psychiatry, if not now . . . When? *Canada's Ment. Hlth,* supplement no. 36, 1963, 1–17.

FURMAN, S. S. Observations on some community mental health programs in Europe. *Amer. J. publ. Hlth*, 1966, 56:202–9.

GOLDFARB, W. Variations in adolescent adjustment of institutionally-reared children. *Amer. J. Orthopsychiat.*, 1947, 17:449–57.

GOODMAN, G. "An Experiment with Companionship Therapy: College Students and Troubled Boys – Assumptions, Selection and Design." Presented at the American Public Health Association Annual Meeting, San Francisco, November 2, 1966.

GRUENBERG, E. M. Application of control methods to mental illness. *Amer. J. publ. Hlth*, 1957, 47:944–52.

—— Can the reorganization of psychiatric services prevent some cases of social breakdown? In STOKES, A. B. (Ed.). *Psychiatry in Transition, 1966–1967.* Toronto: University of Toronto Press, 1967.

—— The prevention of mental disorders. *J. chron. Dis.*, 1959, 9:187–98.

—— (Ed.). Evaluating the effectiveness of mental health services. *Milbank Memorial Fund Quart.*, 1966, 44:part II.

HARLOW, H. F. and M. K. HARLOW. Social deprivation in monkeys. *Scient. American*, 1962, 207:136–46.

HEIDE, H. TER. Migration models and their significance for population forecasts. *Milbank Memorial Fund Quart.*, 1963, 41:56–76.

ILLSLEY, R., A. FINLAYSON, and B. THOMPSON. The motivation and characteristics of internal migrants: A socio-medical study of young migrants in Scotland. Parts I and II. *Milbank Memorial Fund Quart.*, 1963, 41:115–44 and 217–48.

IVES, G. A. Rural community psychiatry. *Canada's ment. Hlth*, 1964, 12:1–3.

JAHODA, M. *Current Concepts of Positive Mental Health.* Joint Commission on Mental Illness and Health Monograph Series no. 1. New York: Basic Books, 1958.

JOINT COMMISSION ON MENTAL ILLNESS AND HEALTH. *Action for Mental Health: Final Report.* New York: Basic Books, 1961.

JOLLY, E. and H. L. BLUM. The role of public health in genetic counselling. *Amer. J. Publ. Hlth*, 1966, 56:186–90.

KEELS, H. S. *et al. A Study of Environmental Stimulation.* University of Iowa Studies in Child Welfare, vol. XV, no. 4. Iowa City: University of Iowa, 1938.

KLEIN, W. *et al. Promoting Mental Health of Older People Through Group Methods: A Practical Guide.* New York: Mental Health Materials Center, 1965.

KOTINSKY, R. and WITMER, H. L. *Community Programs for Mental Health.* Cambridge: Harvard University Press, 1955.

LARSEN, V. L. Stresses of the childbearing years. *Amer. J. publ. Hlth*, 1966, 56:32–36.

LAZARUS, J., B. Z. LOCKE, and D. S. THOMAS. Migration differentials in mental disease. State patterns in first admissions to mental hospitals for all disorders and for schizophrenia, New York, Ohio, and California as of 1950. *Milbank Memorial Fund Quart.*, 1963, 41:25–42.

LEAVELL, H. R. and E. G. CLARK. *Preventive Medicine for the Doctor in the Community: An Epidemiological Approach* (3rd ed.). New York: McGraw-Hill, 1965.

LEE, E. S. Socio-economic and migration differentials in mental disease, New York State, 1949–1951. *Milbank Memorial Fund Quart.*, 1963, 41:249–68.

LEIGHTON, D. C. et al. Psychiatric findings of the Stirling County study. *Amer. J. Psychiat.*, 1963, 119:1021–26.

LEMKAU, P. V. *Mental Hygiene in Public Health* (2nd ed.). New York: McGraw-Hill, 1955.

—— Prevention in psychiatry. *Amer. J. publ. Hlth*, 1965, 55:554–60.

—— Prospects for the Prevention of Mental Illness. *Ment. Hyg.*, 1966, 50:172–79.

—— "The Place of Mental Hygiene in Mental Health." Presented at the meeting of the World Federation for Mental Health, July 19, 1966.

LEWIS, N. D. C. and B. ENGLE. *Wartime Psychiatry: A Compendium of the International Literature.* New York: Oxford University Press, 1954.

LEWIS, W. W. Continuity and intervention in emotional disturbance: A review. *Exceptional Children*, 1965, 31:465–75.

LOCKE, B. Z., G. KRANTZ, and M. KRAMER. Psychiatric need and demand in a prepaid group practice program. *Amer. J. publ. Hlth*, 1966, 56:895–904.

LUNDELL, F. W. and A. M. MANN. Conjoint psychotherapy and marital pairs. *Canad. Med. Ass. J.*, 1966, 94:542–46.

MACKAY R. P. and S. B. WORTIS (Eds.). *Year Books of Neurology, Psychiatry and Neurosurgery, 1950–1966 inclusive.* Chicago: Year Book Medical Publishers, 1950–1966, inclusive.

MASLAND, R. L., S. B. SARASON, and T. GLADWIN. *Mental Subnormality: Biological, Psychological and Cultural Factors.* New York: Basic Books, 1958

McCULLOCH, D. J. Psychiatric seminars for the general practitioner. *Canad. Med. Ass. J.*, 94:235–37, Jan. 29, 1966.

NOYES, A. P. and L. C. KOLB. *Modern Clinical Psychiatry* (6th ed.). Philadelphia: W. B. Saunders, 1963.

OZARIN, L. D. The community mental health center: a public health facility. *Amer. J. publ. Hlth*, 1966, 56:26–31.

PAFFENBARGER, R. S. and L. J. McCABE. The effect of obstetric and prenatal events on risk of mental illness in women of childbearing age. *Amer. J. publ. Hlth*, 1966, 56:400–07.

PENNSYLVANIA MENTAL HEALTH INC. *Mental Health Education: A Critique.* Philadelphia: Pennsylvania Mental Health Inc., May 1960.

PRESIDENT OF THE UNITED STATES. Message from the President of the United States, *Relative to Mental Illness and Mental Retardation.* 88th Congress, House of Representatives Document no. 58, 1963.

ROBERTS, C. A. Major changes in the administration of psychiatric services in Canada. *Canad. Psychiat. Ass. J.*, 1966, 11:228–41.

ROOSENBURG, A. M. "Mental Health Aspects of the Prevention of Crime." Presented at the Third United Nations Congress on the Prevention of Crime and the Treatment of Offenders, Stockholm, August 9–18, 1965. Unpublished.

ROSE, A. *Regent Park: A Study in Slum Clearance.* Toronto: University of Toronto Press, 1958.

SANDERS, D. S. A bookshelf on mental health. *Amer. J. publ. Hlth*, 1965, 55:502–9.

SANDFORD, N. The prevention of mental illness. *Bull. Menninger Clin.*, 1966, 30:1–22.

SCOTT, J. P., E. FREDERICSON, and J. L. FULLER. Experimental exploration of the critical period hypothesis. *Personality*, 1951, 1:162–83.

SHAW, C. R. and H. D. McKAY. *Juvenile Delinquency and Urban Areas.* Chicago: University of Chicago Press, 1942. Chapter 20.

SPITZ, R. "Grief." Film available through New York University Film Library, Washington Square, New York, N.Y.

SROLE, L. *et al. Mental Health in the Metropolis: The Midtown Manhattan Study.* Vol. 1. New York: McGraw-Hill, 1962.

STOGDILL, C. G. School achievement, learning difficulties and mental health. *Canada's ment. Hlth*, supplement 48, vol. 13, no. 5, 1965, pp. 1–18.

SZASZ, T. *The Myth of Mental Illness: Foundations of a theory of personal conduct.* New York: Hoeber-Harper, 1961.

TURNER, W. E. *et al.* "Integration of Mental Health into Public Health Progress: Advantages and Disadvantages." Presented at the American Public Health Association Annual Meeting, November 3, 1966.

TYHURST, J. S. "Prevention: 1966." In STOKES, A. B. (Ed.). *Psychiatry in Transition, 1966–1967.* Toronto: University of Toronto Press, 1967.

—— *et al. More for the Mind: A Study of Psychiatric Services in Canada.* Toronto: Canadian Mental Health Association, 1963.

UNITED STATES DEPARTMENT OF HEALTH, EDUCATION AND WELFARE. S. S. FURMAN, *Community Mental Health Services in Northern Europe.* P.H.S. Publication no. 1407. Washington: Government Printing Office, 1965.

—— *Evaluation in Mental Health.* P.H.S. Publication no. 413. Washington: Government Printing Office, 1955.

WALTER REED ARMY INSTITUTE OF RESEARCH. *Symposium on Preventive and Social Psychiatry*, April 15–17, 1957. Washington: Government Printing Office, 1958.

WORLD HEALTH ORGANIZATION, Technical Report Series, no. 9. *Mental Health: Report of the First Session of the Expert Committee.* Geneva: World Health Organization.

—— No. 31. *Mental Health: Report of the Second Session of the Expert Committee.* Geneva: World Health Organization.

—— No. 73. *The Community Mental Hospital: Third Report of the Expert Committee on Mental Health.* Geneva: World Health Organization.

—— No. 134. *The Psychiatric Hospital as a Center for Preventive Work in Mental Health: Fifth Report of the Expert Committee on Mental Health.* Geneva: World Health Organization.

———— No. 171. *Mental Health Problems of Aging and the Aged: Sixth Report of the Expert Committee on Mental Health.* Geneva: World Health Organization.

———— No. 177. *Social Psychiatry and Community Attitudes: Seventh Report of the Expert Committee on Mental Health.* Geneva: World Health Organization.

———— No. 183. *Mental Health Problems of Automation: Report of a Study Group.* Geneva: World Health Organization.

———— No. 185. *Epidemiology of Mental Disorders: Eighth Report of the Expert Committee on Mental Health.* Geneva: World Health Organization.

———— No. 208. *Undergraduate Teaching of Psychiatry and Mental Health Promotion: Ninth Report of the Expert Committee on Mental Health.* Geneva: World Health Organization.

———— No. 223. *Programme Development in the Mental Health Field: Tenth Report of the Expert Committee on Mental Health.* Geneva: World Health Organization.

———— No. 235. *The Role of Public Health Officers and General Practitioners in Mental Health Care: Eleventh Report of the Expert Committee on Mental Health.* Geneva: World Health Organization.

———— No. 252. *Training of Psychiatrists: Twelfth Report of the Expert Committee on Mental Health.* Geneva: World Health Organization.

———— No. 275. *Psychosomatic Disorders: Thirteenth Report of the Expert Committee on Mental Health.* Geneva: World Health Organization.

ZIMAND, S. (ed.). *Public Health and Welfare: The Citizens' Responsibility. Selected Papers of Homer Folks.* New York: Macmillan, 1958.

ZUBINE, J. and E. I. BURDOCK. "The Revolution in Psychopathology and its Implications for Public Health." Presented at the American Public Health Association Annual Meeting, 6 October, 1964.

PART TWO

Medical Aspects of Primary Prevention of Psychiatric Disorders

CONTRIBUTORS

M. BEISER, M.D., is Assistant Professor of Social Psychiatry, Harvard School of Public Health, Department of Behavioral Sciences, Boston, Massachusetts, U.S.A.

J. D. M. GRIFFIN, M.A., M.D., D.P.M., is General Director, Canadian Mental Health Association, Toronto, Ontario.

B. GOLDBERG, B.SC., M.D., C.M., C.R.C.P.(C), is Superintendent, The Children's Psychiatric Research Institute, and Lecturer in Psychiatry, University of Western Ontario, London, Ontario.

R. C. A. HUNTER, M.D., C.M., C.R.C.P.(C), is Professor and Chairman, Department of Psychiatry, University of Toronto, Toronto, Ontario.

V. A. KRAL, M.D., is Director, Gerontological Unit, Allan Memorial Institute of Psychiatry, and Associate Professor of Psychiatry, McGill University, Montréal, P.Q.

A. LAMBERTI, B.A., M.D., D.P.H., is Director, Children's Psychiatric Services, Royal Ottawa Sanatorium, and Assistant Professor, University of Ottawa, Ottawa, Ontario.

W. HARDING LE RICHE, B.SC., M.D., M.P.H., is Professor and Head, Department of Epidemiology and Biometrics, School of Hygiene, University of Toronto, Toronto, Ontario.

D. G. McKERRACHER, M.D., F.R.C.P.(C), is Head, Department of Psychiatry, University of Saskatchewan, Saskatoon, Saskatchewan.

J. A. RASSELL, M.B., D.P.H., D.PSYCH., is Lecturer in Psychiatry, University of Ottawa, and Psychiatrist, Ottawa Civic Hospital, Ottawa, Ontario.

V. SZYRYNSKI, M.D., PH.D., F.R.C.P.(C), F.A.C.P., F.B.PS.S., F.A.P.A., is Professor of Psychiatry, University of Ottawa, and Head, Department of Psychiatry, Ottawa General Hospital, Ottawa, Ontario.

W. HARDING LE RICHE, M.D.

4 Preventive Programmes in Mental Diseases: Their Evaluation

Caplan (1) points out in his book *Principles of Preventive Psychiatry* that he has made no attempt to differentiate programmes for the prevention of specific mental disorders, because the knowledge for such prevention, except in a few instances, does not exist. It appears, therefore, that a great deal of his book is devoted to what we should do, if we knew what to do. There is, however, a great deal of value in Caplan's approach to the characteristics of crisis in the life experience of people and what might be done, or should be done, to help patients to overcome such serious situations of stress.

The effect of the rise in tension on the functioning of the individual is due partly to its intensity and partly to its duration. The total effect is in four characteristic phases:

Phase 1. The initial rise in tension from the impact of the stimulus calls forth the habitual problem-solving responses of homeostasis.

Phase 2. Lack of success and continuation of stimulus is associated with rise in tension and the previously described stage of upset and ineffectuality.

Phase 3. Further rise in tension takes it past a third threshold when it acts as a powerful internal stimulus in the mobilization of internal and external resources. The individual calls on his reserves of strength and of emergency problem-solving mechanisms. He uses novel methods to attack the problem, which may meanwhile have abated in intensity. He may gradually define the problem in a new way, so that it comes within the range of previous experience. Aspects of the problem which were neglected may now be brought into awareness, with the consequent linking with capacities and accessory problem-solving techniques which were previously neglected as irrelevant. He may now set aside other aspects of the problem as impossible to handle, but not relevant. There may be active resignation and giving up of certain aspects of goals as unattainable. He may explore by trial and error, either in action or in abstract thought, which avenues are open and which closed.

As a result of this mobilization of effort and redefinition of the situation, the problem may be solved. This will usually involve an alteration in the individual's role vis-à-vis his group. Complementarity between him and others which was disturbed during the previous upset is now re-established.

Phase 4. If the problem continues and can neither be solved with need satisfaction nor avoided by need resignation or perceptual distortion, the tension mounts beyond a further threshold or its burden increases over time to a breaking point. Major disorganization of the individual with drastic results then occurs.

The various social and cultural mechanisms, both internal and external, available to the patient, will determine a good or bad result. What we do not know, however, is whether these crisis situations are very important in precipitating serious psychiatric disease. For this reason we must undertake more and better designed epidemiological studies on population groups.

Without going into a great deal of detail on the nature of the epidemiological methods, it suffices to say that in the present setting, that of evaluation of a programme, epidemiological method will be concerned primarily with measurement of those variables which can be measured. We have simplified matters considerably by deliberately stating that our conference is concerned with psychiatric disorders, which presumably can be counted and measured. We have quite wisely stayed away from that interesting and intangible abstraction known as "mental health."

In all clinical medicine, which includes psychiatry, diagnostic accuracy is a prerequisite in any epidemiological study. The disease must be identified and it should be classified. The following listing is from a paper by Kessel (8) in which he discusses the technique of a psychiatric survey.

This classification, important as it is for epidemiological purposes, was designed to suit hospital material. It has been shown greatly to underestimate psychiatric morbidity. The College of General Practitioners has produced its own classification system (Research Committee, Coll. Gen. Pract., 1959) and the psychiatric section of this is appended in a slightly abbreviated form.

1st level:	5	mental, psychoneurotic and personality disorders
2nd level:	51	psychoses
	52	psychoneurotic disorders
	53	other psychogenic illness
3rd level:	5101	schizophrenia
	5102	manic-depressive psychosis
	5103	senile psychosis
	5104	organic psychosis
	5105	other psychoses
	5201	anxiety states without somatic symptoms
	5202	anxiety states with somatic symptoms
	5203	anxiety states with depression
	5204	anxiety states with phobic symptoms
	5205	hysterical reaction

```
5206  asthenic reaction
5207  other unspecified psychoneuroses including rare
      obsessional states
5301  amentia
5302  addictions
5303  psychopathic personality
5304  other psychiatric illness
```

This classification has the great merit that general practitioners can apply it; it is admirably suited for a general morbidity survey but it shares a demerit with the I.C.D. in that the patient with a somatic *complaint* remains more likely to be classified under the appropriate bodily system than into this section. Code 5202 covers such cases but the whole tenor of the classification is none the less to code the worried, dyspeptic patient as "9403: disorder of gastric function" and hence into the diseases of the digestive system.

This is one of the essential differences between the general practitioner's psychiatric patients and those of the psychiatrist. Only about 10% of the practitioner's *psychiatric* patients present with what may be termed psychological symptoms. The majority of the patients with neurotic illnesses (it was shown that 94% of all the psychiatric illnesses encountered by the G.P. were neurotic) present with physical complaints. Moreover they expect somatic diagnoses and treatment. "The general practitioner recognizes such patients in a number of ways: by their demeanour, by the way they describe their complaints, by eliminating pathological processes that might be responsible for these, by his knowledge, often extending over many years, of the patient, his family and his social stresses, and by the elaborate though not specially contrived psychiatric history which he obtains during this time. Although these disabilities must be classified formally as neuroses, the general practitioner sees them in three principal groups. First, there are the patients presenting psychological symptoms such as depression or fatigue; the spontaneity of the presentation of these symptoms should be stressed since with judicious (sometimes injudicious), questioning they can be elicited from most people. The second and largest group comprises a segment of those patients with somatic symptoms which the practitioner does not attribute to organic pathology; a psychogenic factor for the symptoms may or may not be obvious. Thirdly, the elaboration or protraction of recognized physical illness may indicate a psychiatric component."

The emphasis on patients' complaints rather than formal diagnoses arose because making these is not a necessary part of everyday work in the surgery; with a satisfactory case-finding system, the practitioner should have to depart as little as possible from his usual practices. Therefore, although the system used should not ignore diagnoses when these are forthcoming, it should not compel the practitioner to diagnose when he would not.

It could well be realized, therefore, that if measurement is attempted in the field of mental illness, it should be carried out by the same observers. And it should also be clear that these same people, psychiatrists or general physicians, do not function equally well as a measuring instrument every day of the week. For a closer degree of accuracy, therefore, it may be necessary in special studies to have a consensus of at least three physicians. If this is necessary in studying heart murmurs, it is quite clearly imperative in a study of psychiatric disorders.

Having described the need for as high a degree of accuracy as possible in the diagnosis of psychiatric disease the next step is to describe certain of the technical problems associated with various types of surveys and studies on groups of patients. Especially in the field of psychiatric disease, the validity of assessments must be carefully considered and studied long before the particular large study is undertaken. The validity of assessment is an indication of the efficiency of the diagnostic technique. Here we need carefully to compare the findings by a number of psychiatrists, or other observers, on the same patients, in order to clarify their criteria of judgment. So far, few attempts have been made to study the reliability of psychiatric diagnoses (2). In his study on cerebral arteriosclerosis and senile psychosis in Syracuse, New York, Gruenberg used, not psychiatrists or nurses, but specially trained field interviewers who were taught the technique of recording factual objective indicators of disease. This may come as a bit of a blow to psychiatrists and nurses, but it should be remembered that physicians, especially, are trained not merely to observe and describe signs and symptoms, but also to interpret as they proceed. This is why many clinical observations on drugs are far better carried out not by doctors, but by technicians who are merely trained to observe and not to interpret. I am not saying that psychiatrists cannot observe, but some of them may find this function difficult.

Also involved in the question of reliability are subject variation, observer variation, and interaction between the subject and the observer. These matters are well-known to psychiatrists and sociologists, but perhaps not so well to practitioners of public health, who have not in the past carried out many studies on patients themselves. In the future they will increasingly cope with this type of situation. Whereas subject variation is important, many medical people and nurses do not adequately realize that even the most skilled radiologists and pathologists, on examining their own plates and slides on two different occasions, may vary quite alarmingly in their diagnoses. And when two or three or more of these specialists examine the same data, the results are even more chastening. Psychiatrists, who are dealing with what is considerably more intangible than slides or X-ray plates, need considerable experience in the testing of their own reliability before embarking on any large-scale studies. At that point they can devise and develop standardized diagnoses and questionnaire techniques. Even if these diagnostic procedures have been determined for reliability, they should also be tested for validity. In other words, what meaning do they have over a period of time in the same patient? (4)

What is also needed is a serious long-term study of the natural history of mental disease. Another method, even more difficult, consists of the empirical analysis of the various phenomena which must be observed before a particular diagnosis is reached. This is also involved in the whole process of evaluation.

Most of us will be mainly concerned with survey studies of various types, although we should also discuss other sources of data such as death certificate material, existing data such as hospital, police, and social agency records (12).

DEATH CERTIFICATE MATERIAL

These data are often very limited, as the cause of death may not describe the mental condition of the patient. A patient suffering from senile psychosis will commonly have a death certificate which ascribes his death to arteriosclerosis, myocardial infarct, or cerebral thrombosis. In the case of suicide, however, the chances of obtaining a true cause of death are greater than in the example provided above.

1. *Calculation of death rates in a changing population*

In the study of suicide, for example, the comparison of risks, which is the essence of the observational approach in epidemiology, consists simply in calculating and comparing death-rates. These are defined as the number of deaths from a specified cause per 1000 persons exposed to the risk of dying during a period of time in a particular subgroup of the population. In this fundamental ratio of "cases" to "exposure to risk," the estimation of the latter is frequently imprecise. Two methods of calculating the exposure to risk are commonly used, and both involve the notion that the total exposure combines the number of persons exposed and the duration of their exposure. In vital statistical death-rates, the average number of people alive at the middle of the time-period are assumed to have been exposed to the risk of death during the whole of that period. When dealing with large groups of patients, e.g., in industries, this mid-year population can be simply estimated by averaging the population routinely estimated at the beginning and end of the year.

Although appropriate enough for the relatively stable numbers of major population groups, this simple technique may be less effective when dealing with a population, such as the patients in a large mental hospital, whose size is changing erratically over the period of observation. In these circumstances, the total number of months and years lived by each individual who was a member of the group for all or part of the period of observation are added. This gives an "exposure to risk" (usually expressed in terms of the total person-months or person-years of exposure) which can then be used as a sound basis for the calculation of the death-rate.

An extension of this concept of totalling the person-years of exposure is applicable when follow-up observations over longer than a year are being made on closed groups such as large groups of families living in certain conditions. In these studies, whether of mortality or morbidity, the focus of interest is on the relative risks of death or onset of mental illness after the beginning of the period of observation. With the steadily wasting population under review these numbers of deaths, recoveries, or relapses will be much affected by the falling numbers exposed to risk. Some systematic allowance must be made for this in the analysis of the results of any follow-up procedure. In practice, a very simple modification of the actuarial life-table is used. Table I sets out a hypothetical example of this technique. Suppose we start with 1250 individuals under observation. During the course of the first year of follow-up, 60 die and 40 are lost from observation because they have left the district or for other reasons. The 1150 who survive under review at the end of the first year obviously contribute one year each to the total person-years of exposure for that first year. It is then assumed that the remaining 100 who have been lost to observation, either through death or migration, were exposed to risk for an average of half the period, i.e., for six months. These 100 thus contribute $100 \times 1/2$ year $= 50$ person-years of exposure to the grand total. The same adjustment is made for the 1150 survivors and 100 losses in the second and again in the same way for succeeding years of the follow-up.

TABLE I

THE CALCULATION OF DEATH-RATES IN A CHANGING POPULATION [REID 12]

Year of observation	Initial population	No. dying	No. withdrawn	Total exposure in man-years	Death-rate/ 1,000 man-years
1	1,250	60	40	1,200	50
2	1,150	20	80	1,100	18
3	1,050	12	68	1,010	12

Once the total exposure to risk in each year is available, two courses lie open. If the material is large enough to give reasonably stable rates, the risks of death in each year of follow-up can be calculated as before by expressing the annual number of deaths per 1000 person-years of exposure in the appropriate year. The trend in mortality with duration of exposure in two different sets of circumstances can then be directly compared. More often, however, there is neither enough material for statistical stability nor any very appropriate similar experience available for comparison. In this event, it is often worth while comparing the mortality experience of the particular survey with national or other standard death-rates. Buck (1955), for example, compared the number of deaths from cardiovascular disease among hospital patients with functional psychoses observed over a period of years with the number to be expected on death-rates for the whole Canadian population during the same time. For each age-grouping of patients, the total number of person-years of exposure are worked out as already indicated. Then the age-specific death-rates, e.g., from coronary heart disease, are applied to this total to obtain the total number of deaths from the disease which would have occurred among these patients had they suffered the same coronary mortality experience as the rest of their compatriots. The number of deaths observed is conveniently expressed as a ratio (%) of the number expected at standard rates (12).

2. *The need for standardization of rates*

As there is a differing age and sex distribution of the major mental disorders, methods must be used which summarize the experience of whole populations with different age-sex structures. Here we use the direct and indirect methods of standardization of rates for age and sex.

In epidemiological studies of smaller groups [Reid 12] indirect methods of standardization are more appropriate, since the smaller numbers involved make any age-specific mortality or morbidity rates calculated from them very subject to random variation. The principle and method involved are most simply illustrated in the standardized mortality ratio used in the study of deaths among occupational groups.

In Table II, the age- and sex-specific rates in some large standard experience, as in all employed males in the country, are applied to the total number of persons in the corresponding age-group in the particular population being surveyed. This gives the number of deaths to be expected in a population of that size, age, and sex constitution had they experienced the same age- and sex-specific death-rates as the standard population. In the age-group 25–34, for example, 10,151 doctors were exposed to risk for the five-year period 1949–1953, i.e., a total exposure of 50,755 man-years. Had they suffered the same suicide rate as all employed men of their age (80 per 1,000,000 per annum), 4 suicides would have occurred instead of the 16 actually observed. The process is repeated for each age- and sex-group and the total number of expected deaths thus obtained. The total number of deaths actually observed is then usually expressed as a ratio per cent. to the total expected number for the age-range 20–64 years.

TABLE II

COMPUTATION OF A STANDARDIZED SUICIDE RATIO FOR DOCTORS* [REID 12]

Years	Census population 1951	Registered suicides 1949–1953	National death-rates per 1,000,000 per annum	Expected no. of suicides 1949–1953
20–24	1,053		60	
25–34	10,151	16	80	4
35–44	9,747	17	124	6
45–54	8,290	19	218	9
55–64	4,879	9	324	8
		—		—
		61		27

$$\text{Standard mortality ratio} = \frac{\text{Observed deaths}}{\text{Expected deaths}} \times 100 = \frac{6,100}{27} = 226 \text{ per cent.}$$

*Data from Occupational Mortality Supplement, Registrar General, England and Wales, 1958.

In this way, the overall experience of the particular group is compared to the standard, after differences in the age and sex structure of the populations have been taken into account. This indirect form of standardization is mainly used in the study of the occupational or social distribution of death in adult populations, but it can equally serve in the analysis of disabling sickness due to diseases of psychological origin or with psychic manifestations.

Useful as these summary indices of death or sickness may be in the study of long-term trends in disease among populations where the age structure is changing considerably over the period, their use should not be allowed to obscure important features of the data. The age- and sex-specific rates should always be calculated and their pattern inspected. In the example of suicides among doctors, for instance, the excess among this occupational group is most marked in the younger age-groups – suggesting that initial selection rather than occupational conditions determines the unduly high suicide-rate among the profession. At the same time, the actual numbers upon which such a conclusion is based must be detailed, so that their significance can be assessed. A useful rule of thumb is to test whether the observed number of deaths is within sampling limits given by twice the square root of the expected number. In the age-group 45–54, for example, the 19 deaths registered exceed the 9 deaths expected by more than the chance limits of $\pm 2\sqrt{9} = 6$ deaths (12).

3. *Social and occupational factors in mortality*

It suffices to say, in this connection, that social class, income, and occupation are variables which must be taken into account in studying deaths associated with psychopathology. The condition commonly studied in this connection is suicide. An interesting approach here is to compare married women with their husbands, for the social class gradient is kept constant. This type of mortality study is also important in those diseases designated as "psychosomatic." But here we get into great difficulties regarding definition and diagnosis.

4. *Difficulties in interpreting mortality data*

Death certificate data are not easy to interpret in the mental diseases, as in many cases the mental condition concerned may not be mentioned at all the death certificate. Also, fashions change in regard to death certificates, and differing diagnostic terms are used in different parts of the world. If we study occupations, these may vary considerably during the lifetime of a particular person, thus almost nullifying comparisons. In all this there is a selective process. For instance, excessive suicide rates, or admissions to mental hospital, from the poorer parts of a city, need not imply that poverty causes these situations. It may well be that patients with these predispositions drifted into more poorly paid jobs, because of an inability to cope with more demanding environments.

HOSPITAL, SOCIAL AGENCY, AND POLICE RECORDS

In the present presentation we will use hospital records as a model in this type of study, assuming that the other types of readily available records could be used in the same manner.

An excellent recent study on long-stay patients in Canadian mental hospitals in the period 1955–1963, by Richman (13) is well worth reading. He carefully discusses problems in evaluation of mental disease in institutions. Some of his conclusions are that during the period under review the average number of in-patients in Canadian mental hospitals decreased by 6 per cent, while hospital days per 1,000 population also decreased, from 1,152 to 898. Marked reductions have taken place during this period in the ratio of patients with psychoses to the general population. There has been a relative reduction in those aged 35–44 who had been in hospital from two to five years. It would appear feasible to have a reduction of the mental-hospital population to 1.5 per 1,000 population by 1971, according to Richman. Why this change has taken place is a matter for further study. Presumably, new drug therapy must have had some influence, although the falling trends have been observed in certain countries for some years. The other publications of Richman should be carefully read, especially by those Cassandras who believe that our population is increasingly becoming less sane.

CERTAIN CONCEPTS IN
MEASUREMENT OF MENTAL MORBIDITY

As Dorn (5) has shown, there are three basic units in the measurement of morbidity: the persons who are ill, the periods or spells of illnesses that they experience, and the duration of such illnesses. The following discussion is from Reid (12):

The term "spells" will have a meaning which depends on the context: thus it may refer either to a stay in hospital or to a period off work. The frequency of illness can be looked at from two points of view: illnesses commencing during a defined period, or illnesses in existence at any time during a defined period. In the first instance, the usual practice is to define "incidence," either in terms of persons or of spells, as the rate at which illnesses commence during a defined period among the corresponding population exposed to the risk of doing so. The incidence (attack or inception) rate is thus:

$$\frac{\text{No. of new cases beginning during a defined period of time}}{\text{Average number in a defined population exposed to risk during that time}} \times 1000$$

The precise definition of "new illness or case" will depend on the circumstances of its use. In hospital statistics, it will mean a first admission, in social security systems a claim for benefit. In health survey work, where a pre-existing illness is discovered, the date of discovery rather than the date of onset will bring the patient into the numerator of the incidence rate as a "new case" in a defined period of time. Analogous arguments hold for the measures of point and period prevalence. Because of past inconsistencies in the usage of these terms, reports of surveys or other studies should give a detailed account of the conventions used.

The point prevalence rate is commonly taken as:

$$\frac{\text{No. of cases ill at one point in time}}{\text{Defined population exposed to risk at that time}} \times 1000$$

As Dorn points out, this rate is not realistic when the period of observation cannot be one instant in time. Where this period is relatively short, however, the conventional point prevalence rate is an adequate measure of the frequency of existing disease in the community at one point in time. The actual level will depend, of course, on the clinical grading of the activity and severity of disease required for acceptance as a "case," e.g., on the need for medical consultation or hospital care. When the period of observation is longer than one day – in the Baltimore study reported by Lemkau it was as long as a year – the "prevalence" rate is strictly the number of clinically active cases counted at the beginning of the period plus those becoming active during the whole period of observation divided by the average number exposed to risk during that time, or of the population at the midpoint of the period. This may be conveniently referred to as a "period prevalence rate."

In mental disorders such as the psychoneuroses, where acute symptoms and occupational disability may occur in the same individual at varying intervals, a clear distinction must be made between "persons" and "attacks" or "spells." In the statistics of social insurance agencies, for example, one person may have several "spells" of absence from work for psychoneurotic illness during the course of the year. In these circumstances, the same conventions in principle are used as before but the numerators are modified thus:

Point prevalence – Number of spells of sickness current at point in time
(spells)
Period prevalence – number of spells which are current *at some time*
(spells)   during the defined period of observation.

The duration of illness, however defined, can be measured or expressed either as (1) the days of illness per person among the population exposed to risk during the defined period; (2) the total days of illness per sick person; or (3) total days of illness per spell of illness.

As before, the definition of the beginning and ending of each individual spell of "illness" will depend on the context. The choice of the measure used will depend on the needs of the particular study.

However morbidity is measured, the aim of the methods used is to establish the rates at which new cases of mental disorder are occurring in the varying conditions of human populations, and how the evolution of the disease is affected by changing circumstances. In other words, we are trying to describe the pattern of disease, not in static, but in dynamic terms – a concept to be remembered in any discussion of the value of sickness data from any source.

In surveys of chronic disabling disease like schizophrenia, it is often profitable to express the end-result of the accumulation of such disease in any given population in terms of the "life-expectancy" of the disease for any individual born into such a group. This "disease-expectancy" or "morbid risk" means the likelihood that any individual, who survives long enough to be exposed during the period of risk in life when the particular disease usually arises, will develop the disease. This period of risk varies from disease to disease: in schizophrenia, for example, it is usually taken to be between the ages of 15 and 45. Probably the most widely used method of calculating those morbid risks is that due to Weinberg. It has the merit of simplicity, as the following hypothetical example will show. From a census-type of survey at one point in time, the age and sex distribution of the population surveyed and the number of mentally ill individuals might be ascertained, with results as in Table III. It is assumed that all affected individuals can be identified by the diagnostic methods used.

TABLE III

CALCULATION OF "DISEASE-EXPECTANCY RATE" OR
"MORBID RISK" [REID 12]

Male population surveyed

Age structure			
		Schizophrenia cases found =	23
		Total population surveyed =	5,000
0–14	1,500	*less* pre-risk-period males =	1,500
15–24	900		————
25–34	800		3,500
35–44	700	*less* 1/2 risk-period	
45–54	500	population (15–44)	
55+	600	1/2 (900 + 800 + 700) =	1,200
	————		————
Total	5,000	Adjusted population at risk	2,300

$$\text{"Disease-expectancy rate" or "morbid risk"} = \frac{23}{2,300} \times 100 = 1.0\%$$

To estimate the total exposure to risk during the period of 15–45 years of age, the number of males who have not yet reached the lower age-limit of 15 years (1500) is subtracted from the total number surveyed (5000), of whom 1100 have already passed through the risk period. The males still within the age-limits at the time of census are assumed to be fairly evenly spread throughout the period and to have been exposed on the average for one half of it. Half of their total (1200) is therefore subtracted from the preceding residual to give an adjusted population exposed to risk of 2300. The "disease-expectancy" or "morbid risk" is then found by expressing the number of cases of schizophrenia alive in the whole population (23) to the adjusted population as a rate per cent (1.0%). The whole operation can be summarized by the formula:

$$p^* = \frac{a}{b - (b_0 + \frac{1}{2}b_m)}$$

where p^* = morbid risk
a = number affected

b = total population surveyed
b_0 = number who have not yet reached the
period of manifestation
and b_m = number within specific age-limits

Within limits imposed by the small percentages usually found, the usual standard errors of proportional rates can be used to test the significance of the difference between any two such morbid risks in different populations.

TYPES OF SURVEY STUDY IN MENTAL DISORDERS

1. *Comprehensive area surveys*

While a great deal of work has been done in this field, the problem of validity in field studies of psychological disorder remains ever present. In an excellent recent review (4), evidence of validity in most studies was found to be scant. The main conclusion reached is that the lowest socio-economic stratum has the highest rate of symptomatology. Well-known studies in this area are those by Hollingshead and Redlich (7), D. C. Leighton *et al.* (10) and A. H. Leighton *et al.* (9). The last is cross-cultural, in that it studies the Yoruba people in Nigeria, comparing them with Canadians in Sterling County, Nova Scotia. Another well-known study of this type is the Midtown Study in New York (15).

2. *Selected group surveys*

Without going into great detail, it may be convenient and useful to study certain groups: students, military conscripts, or industrial workers, for psychological disease. A great deal of useful information can be obtained from such studies, provided that suitable controls be found and that great attention be paid to comparability of diagnostic techniques.

Cobb *et al.* (3), working in industrial groups, regard certain aspects of mental disease in terms of social maladjustment, illness, hysteria, neurosis, and antisocial behaviour. In their view, those with neurotic tendencies do not become part of the problem unless the environment is such as to elicit inappropriate or disfunctional behaviour. They rightly relate many sources of social maladjustment such as lowered self-esteem, or low status in a company hierarchy, to sickness. Quite clearly, this type of situation can be studied, but what is to be done in the preventive sense is certainly not clear. Everyone cannot be a chief, as there must always be many Indians! It is interesting that these observers regard reduced communication between workers and management as being the beginning of antisocial behaviour on the part of management.

The area under discussion does not include the major psychoses, but it does cover common situations in day-to-day human interaction. It seems that in these situations a great deal of research work can be done. For instance, it was found that foremen in a particular industrial setting had a considerably larger prevalence of peptic ulcers than the workmen whom they supervised. The reasons for this could be investigated by medical and psychological means. Measurement and good design of studies would be of great importance in such investigations.

It could well be that conflict and wear-and-tear, both physical and mental, are the price we must pay for Cadillacs and colour television. If this is so, we should at least try to discover the mechanisms of such a situation. Possibly we might be able at least to mitigate certain particular episodes of illness and unrest. Perhaps industrial strikes may be socially therapeutic while financially disruptive, if such situations were to be studied in terms of illness at such times.

3. *Longitudinal Investigations*

As we clearly realize that prevalence studies are difficult to carry out and to plan, an ideal design would be a long-term longitudinal design in which groups of people are observed over a period of time. Problems of sampling may be quite complex in studies of this type. A great difficulty in longitudinal studies in highly mobile societies is that one fairly easily loses track of people in the original sample. Important selective influences relative to psychological disease may be missed. Nevertheless, these studies must be undertaken if we are to learn anything new and constructive about mental disease.

DISCUSSION

What we have tried to describe in the present paper are certain of the methods of approach which should be used in the evaluation of programes said to be useful in the prevention of mental disease. We need to stress that very little is known of the prevention of the major psychoses. Much more is known about the prevention and treatment of mental effect of chemical intoxications and addictions, the effects of head trauma, infection, and tumour of the brain, and symptomatic psychoses associated with other diseases such as nutritional deficiency and thyroid disease (11).

When we get to those vague borderlands between psychology, sociology, and criminology, we find, in certain academic circles, much heat but little light, and smoke and smokescreens in profusion. This foggy state should be dispelled by clear thought and sound research.

It is, for instance, easy to postulate that there is a continuum between what Taylor and Chave (16) call sub-clinical neurosis, through neurosis, to psychosis. Examination of the facts, however, suggests that this is not by any means the case. These workers point out, and psychiatric clinical experience confirms, that psychosis very often comes as a complete surprise to all concerned, although the family history may be positive, with some personal previous psychotic attacks. Taylor and Chave found, from their work, that the hypothesis of a continuum does not stand up to experience. On the contrary, psychosis and neurosis operate in opposing directions. A fascinating result of their work is the suggestion that environment may have a stronger influence, both positive and negative, in psychotic illness. This means that many more studies of the type suggested by these workers should be carried out, with due respect to validity and proper statistical design. But in the meanwhile, *More for the Mind* has many sound suggestions which should be considered now.

REFERENCES

1. CAPLAN, G. *Principles of Preventive Psychiatry.* New York: Basic Books, 1964
2. CARSTAIRS, G. M. Some targets for future epidemiological research, in J. D. N. HILL (6).
3. COBB, S. *et al.* An environmental approach to mental health. *Annals New York acad. Science,* 1963, 107:596–606.
4. DOHRENWEND, B. P. and B. S. DOHRENWEND. The problem of validity in field studies of psychological disorder. *J. abnormal psychol.,* 1965, 70: 52–69.
5. DORN, H. F. A Classification System for Morbidity Concepts. *Pub. hlth. Rep.,* 1957, 72:1043–48.
6. HILL, J. D. N. *et al. The Burden on the Community: The Epidemiology of Mental Illness, A Symposium. Nuffield Provincial Hospitals Trust,* Toronto: Oxford University Press, 1962.
7. HOLLINGSHEAD, A. B. and F. C. REDLICH. *Mental Disease and Social Class* New York: *Cornell University Press,* 1963.
8. KESSEL, W. I. N. Conducting a psychiatric survey in general practice in J. D. N. HILL (6).
9. LEIGHTON, A. H. *et al. Psychiatric Disorder Among the Yoruba.* Ithaca, New York: John Wiley, 1958.
10. LEIGHTON, D. C. *et al. The Character of Danger.* New York: Basic Book, 1963.
11. MAYER-GROSS, W. *et al. Clinical Psychiatry.* London: Cassell, 1960.
12. REID, D. D. *Epidemiological Methods in the Study of Mental Disorders.* Public Health Papers. No. 2. Geneva: World Health Organization, 1960.
13. RICHMAN, A. Long-stay patients in Canadian mental hospitals, 1955–1963. Canad. med. assoc. J. 1966, 95: 337–49.
14. SCHUMAN, L. M. (Ed.). Research methodology and potential in community health and preventive medicine. *Annals New York acad. Science,* 1963, 107, Art 2: 471–808.

15. SROLE, L. *et al. Mental Health in the Metropolis: The Midtown Study.* New York: McGraw-Hill, 1962. Vol. I.
16. TAYLOR, LORD and S. CHAVE. *Mental Health and Enivronment.* London: Longmans, 1964.
17. TYHURST, J. S. *et al. More for the Mind: A Study of Psychiatric Services in Canada.* Toronto: 1963. Canadian Mental Health Association.

MORTON BEISER, M.D.

5   Primary Prevention of Mental Illness:
     General v. Specific Approaches

In recent years, psychiatry and public health have moved closer together
on many fronts. Parallel with this development there has been increasing concern with certain aspects of prevention. In a broad way, we
might rephrase these concerns as questions, the first in terms of the
proper focus of preventive efforts; the second, of techniques to be
employed.

THE FOCUS OF PREVENTIVE EFFORTS:
WHAT SHALL WE TRY TO PREVENT?

1. *The "specific" focus*
   Programmes of prevention are often directed towards a particular
disease – tuberculosis, cholera, polio, and so forth. There is also interest
in areas where the boundaries are less discrete, for example, cancer
and heart disease. In these latter cases we are really dealing with more
general groupings, and it would be prudent, as some authors have
suggested, to speak of the "cancers" and the "heart diseases." In all
these areas there is an attempt to be as specific as possible about the
focus. Very general categories, for instance "physical illness," have
little utility in preventive work. It would be difficult to imagine someone
talking meaningfully about a programme meant to prevent all diseases.
   In the area of mental illness we have some categories which approach
the level of discreteness of the heart diseases. Granted that groupings
such as "the organic brain syndromes" and "the schizophrenias" may
reflect as much ignorance as knowledge, these at least seem to be
relatively circumscribed and homogeneous categories and are helpful
in clinical and epidemiological work. What, on the other hand, are we to
do with "mental illness" or "psychiatric disorder"? Are these, like
"physical illness," essentially useless constructs in preventive work, even
though they occur repeatedly in the titles of these proceedings?

Several other papers have emphasized, and rightly, that "mental illness" is a particularly troublesome term. We must remember that what we call mental illness is not a unitary phenomenon. This term has come to cover a wide range of heterogeneous phenomena which may bear little or no relationship to each other. In addition, the use of the word "illness" implies a concept of disease which may have very little relevance for some, if not all, categories of psychiatric disorder.

The advocate of a specific approach would be likely to say that it is better to think of discrete problems such as mental retardation, brain syndrome, and schizophrenia, for the following reasons:

1. These conditions fit the disease model more closely than other phenomena which are sometimes labeled mental illness. These latter phenomena (and here we would include neuroses, character disorders, and sociopathic disorders) might be thought of as difficulties of living and might be considered the more legitimate province of jurists, educators, social engineers, welfare workers, and so forth, rather than psychiatrists and public-health workers.

2. A specific approach leads to less fuzziness in conceptualizing problems. While a category such as mental deficiency presents its own difficulties of definition, certainly the margins are easier to draw, the circumscribed area more homogeneous than if we choose to think of a category as broad and ill-defined as "mental illness."

3. With more homogeneous groups of phenomena, it is easier to study questions of etiology, to map out programmes of prevention, and to evaluate the results of such programmes upon discrete, dependent variables (1).

2. The "general" focus

These are powerful arguments, and they have the added appeal of stressing purity and precision, values which are at a high premium in our age. However, there are serious limitations to this approach. While it may be more satisfying to limit our dealings to categories which are easier to define and about which our knowledge is based on firmer ground, such as mental deficiency or organic syndromes, the question of whether or not to do so is largely academic.

Psychiatry as a profession has adopted a large domain of phenomena, many of which fall into the fuzzy area. This is reflected in the psychiatric nomenclature. While there is a great deal of space devoted to conditions which most easily fit the disease model, such as psychosis and brain syndrome, there is progressively more space allotted to phenomena which are considered to be "psychogenic" in origin, such as the patterns of depression and anxiety which we call the neuroses, and the asthma, peptic ulcers, and skin conditions we call psychophysiologic disorders. We also find, creeping into the literature, evidence of concern with phenomena in which the balance of etiological factors seems weighted in the direction of current situational determinants. (This is in distinction to the "psychogenic" model which stresses symptoms as the result of conflicts, which in turn have their origin in childhood experiences.) Such terms as "adjustment reaction," "migration syndrome," "war neurosis," and "institutional neurosis" connote an extension of the field of psychiatric disorders to include phenomena which are probably of a very different order from organic brain syndromes and psychoses. We are here considering aberrant behaviours and reactions to stress. In the case of war neuroses, for example, the disturbed behaviour is a reaction to catastrophic overstimulation of the personality system; in the case of institutional neurosis, the reaction is to a depriving social environment such as "the back ward" of a mental hospital.

This extension of boundaries is not merely an expression of enthusiasm, warranted or not, on the part of mental-health professionals. The general public has given the mental-health professions a mandate to deal in these fuzzy areas.

3. *Establishing a domain*

Does this mean then that the whole question of what we are supposed to prevent is not just general, but so diluted and so ephemeral that we have nowhere to begin? It is probably true that we have no satisfactory definition of "mental illness," and that we should develop a new term for the set of problems encompassed, but the situation may not be so bleak as it appears at first glance. Questions such as "what is mental illness"? and "when is behaviour pathological and when is it a variation of normal"? have been ceaselessly debated. Characteristic of such debates is that they tend to be almost Talmudic in their intricacy and in the tradition that they be carried out in the abstract; they are often only distantly related to actual studies or evidence; and are usually non-productive.

A problem which seems to concern everyone, for instance, is that, as the mental health professions study more and more behaviours, more people will become "psychiatric cases." In the end, if everything from a paraprax to a psychosis is considered "psychiatric," then everyone will qualify as being a case. Psychiatric disorder will then be a category which does not categorize. Such are the conclusions which emanate from arm-chair philosophizing.

Perhaps it would be more productive to recall old axioms, to remember that there are people with disorders of various kinds in society and to ask how to learn from them. In such a context, we would be interested to know if it is possible to define a population of what most people, or at least mental health experts, would consider "psychiatric cases." If this were possible, we might then be able to derive items of behaviour in an empirical, rather than a philosophical fashion, items which would not only characterize our "cases" but would also distinguish them from "normals."

Psychiatrists, in their clinical practices, have been exposed to populations who have defined themselves or have been defined by others as "psychiatric cases." What would happen if we asked these "experts" to interview a "normal" or non-institutional population? In such an instance, there would be no prior definitions of caseness such as there are in mental hospitals and clinics and these experts would be forced to take into account a broader range of behaviours and contexts than their work ordinarily requires. If, in spite of these problems, they succeeded in agreeing on a population of "psychiatric cases" and this did not include everyone they interviewed, this would be a decided advance on a vexing problem. We would have an operationally defined population exhibiting "psychiatric disorder," and this would hopefully give rise to meaningful discussion of this "general" area.

The Harvard Program in Social Psychiatry (formerly the Cornell Program in Social Psychiatry, directed by Alexander H. Leighton) has been concerned with the epidemiology of mental illness and therefore also with problems of definition and boundaries. We have been particularly concerned with the question of when a person is to be considered a psychiatric case and when he is to be considered normal and healthy. A four-point rating system has been devised for use by psychiatrists in evaluating individuals. The points are labeled A, B, C, and D. The psychiatrist will assign an A rating when he is certain that he is dealing with an individual who is a psychiatric case. B means he is probably a psychiatric case, but the psychiatrist cannot be sure with the evidence that he has available. D means he is almost certainly well, and C is a residual category.

As part of an ongoing research project known as the Stirling County Study, a probability sample of 284 adults in nine communities in rural Nova Scotia was interviewed. In the first phase of the research these people were interviewed by means of structured questionnaires. A team of psychiatrists then made independent ABCD ratings based on these questionnaires and other relevant data. The independent ratings obtained in this manner agreed most satisfactorily. During another phase of the research, a sub-sample was interviewed, this time face to face, by another group of psychiatrists using an unstructured, clinical approach. These psychiatrists then made independent evaluations, using the four-category system. The agreement between these ratings and those obtained on the basis of questionnaire data was again satisfactory. It seems possible, then, to obtain consensus by a group of experts about an individual's "caseness." It should be emphasized that these psychiatrists were widely divergent in background and major interests, having in common only a basic training (three years of residency) in clinical psychiatry (2).

Of the total sample of 284, 107 individuals, or 38 per cent, were rated "A." This figure of 38 per cent must be viewed with some reservations. To begin with, the sample can be viewed only with caution as representative of anything beyond the nine communities. These communities were selected for theoretical reasons rather than as being representative of Stirling County or the entire province. A small percentage of Stirling County are of the Negro race; however, the Negro communities have been excluded from the analysis for various reasons. For a discussion of more of the theoretical issues, see D. C. Leighton *et al.* (3).

In the accompanying table, the A category is broken down by distribution of prominent diagnoses. Evidently A, the certain category, contains an extremely heterogeneous collection of disorders. In spite of this heterogeneity, consensus is possible about whether or not an individual should be considered a "psychiatric case."

4. *The Magnitude of the problem*

The second column of this table touches on a different point. In this column, we see the distribution of diagnostic categories in the total sample of 284 individuals. This underscores the magnitude of the problem and also points up the kinds of phenomena with which we would be concerned in a programme aimed at preventing "psychiatric disorders."

This table is based upon a survey of untreated prevalence, and therefore, syndromes such as psychosis and organic brain disorder, which are likely to lead to hospitalization, are probably underrepresented. Even allowing for this underrepresentation, however, it seems clear that most of the psychiatric disorders in these communities are of the psychoneurotic, psychophysiologic, character disorder, and conduct disorder variety. Thus, the majority of categories making up this 38 per cent are those which fit the traditional disease model least well, in

TABLE I

TOTAL SAMPLE: 284; TOTAL A'S: $\dfrac{107}{284} = 38\%$

	Percentage		Occurrence	
Distribution of diagnostic categories[1]	A's (n = 107)		total sample (n = 284)	
Chronic Brain Syndrome	7		3	
Psychosis	0		0	
Psychoneurosis:				
alone	48		18	
with personality disorder	14		5	
with significant psychophysiological disorder[2]	10		4	
with conduct disorder[3]	6		2	
TOTAL Psychoneurosis		78		29
Alcoholism	7		3	
Mental Deficiency[4]	8		3	
TOTAL	100		38	

[1]We do not include such terms as "adjustment reaction." These terms are not true diagnoses, in that there are no descriptive elements, only a statement etiology and prognosis.

[2]Mainly peptic ulcer, asthma, colitis, hypertension. It should be noted that those people with psychophysiological disorders, but no clear evidence of neurosis, psychosis, etc. were classified as B, given the present state of our knowledge.

[3]Mainly sexual acting-out behaviour.

[4]This is probably an underrepresentation. Since the procedure did not include IQ testing, the psychiatrists were forced to err on the side of conservatism.

which the boundary between medical and social is the fuzziest and in which our notions of etiology are the least well founded.

It can be seen, however, that if we followed the admonitions of those who favour a specific approach, we would be led to neglect a large number of troubled people in a community. If we were to follow this course, we would be guilty of a definite error of omission. We might call this the error of neglecting the significant in the service of the elegant.

THE TECHNIQUES OF PREVENTION:
HOW SHALL WE DO IT?

1. *Prevention and social distance*

There is a second way in which one might think of a general versus a specific approach. In public-health practice, a general approach emphasizes the importance of such matters as ensuring adequate diet, the promotion of adequate exercise and rest, and other such measures devoted to the general promotion of good health and resistance to disease. Immunizing a person against diphtheria is an example of "specific" prevention.

It is difficult to adapt this particular model to that of the primary prevention of psychiatric disorders, but I think such an adaptation can be attempted by using the concept of social distance. Social distance can be used to describe human relationships. Those relationships which are quantitatively and qualitatively intense are seen as short. The shortest social distance would be involved, for instance, in the mother-child relationship. If one can consider social distance as a continuum, it is possible to see the doctor-patient, the nurse-patient, the social worker-client, and the teacher-pupil, relationships as being further along this continuum but relatively close to the "short" end. The programmes described by Drs. Griffin, Szyrynski, and McKerracher, involve these combinations in various ways, and they might be categorized as "specific" for the purpose of this presentation. A programme which emphasizes work with an entire community would obviously involve long social distances and would thus be classified as a general programme.

2. *Three aspects of prevention*

During this conference preventive psychiatry as a whole has been considered under three broad headings: (1) control of the physical environment, (2) control of the psychological environment, (3) crisis intervention. In considering the physical environment, there have, for example, been recommendations involving better prenatal services, and consultations by a mental-health expert with pediatricians, obstetricians, and public-health nurses who can deal directly with their clients around the issues of adequate care and the avoidance of infections and injuries. Approaches to the control of the psychological environment have included programmes of education about the effects of maternal deprivation during critical development phases, the relief of intrafamilial tensions, and the early diagnosis and treatment of personality problems in parents. All of these are seen as attempts at primary prevention in that the noxious influences on personality development are avoided or kept to a minimum. Primary prevention as appropriate intervention when people face crises evoked by current situations has also been discussed.

In all these programmes, the common element is that attention is directed to factors affecting the psychological equilibrium of the individual. Preventive efforts in essence extend along short social distances. Lemkau sums up the argument for a specific approach in the following manner: "It is this basis of the increase of individual health making for an increase in the total health of the whole world that public health adheres to for the most part. It is on the basis of this philosophy that greater attention is given in public mental hygiene to relatively short social distances . . . than to broader community and cultural issues" (4).

3. *Three aspects of prevention and the sociocultural milieu*

At the level of community and cultural issues the advocates of specific and general programmes part company. A general approach is a broader approach, aimed not only at individuals, but at the community itself, and it thus involves long social distances. In this frame of reference, a community is conceived of as a quasi organism with a series of interdependent and interrelated parts, the whole, however, being greater than the mere sum of these parts.

The research interests of the Harvard Program in Social Psychiatry have been founded upon this type of thinking. That is, the approach does not give its main emphasis to discrete experiental factors such as (*a*) at the physical level, dietary insufficiencies during pregnancy, (*b*) at the psychological level, loss of a parent, or (*c*) a crisis precipitated by a loss of a job, but rather to the functional state of the whole environmental system.

In this frame of reference, communities are seen in a metaphorical sense as semi-organic systems that perform various functions upon which the survival and well being of the group depends. A social system which functions adequately will satisfy the needs of the majority of its members: acquisition of food, shelter, and other material necessities, the organization and distribution of work, the indoctrination of children into the ways of the system, the use of leisure time, and so forth.

Communities seem to vary in the degree to which they satisfy these requirements and, therefore, in the degree to which they function adequately as social systems. When a system fails to function, we have called this sociocultural disintegration; when a community evidences good functioning, we have called it socioculturally integrated (5).

A number of communities which vary on a sociocultural integration-disintegration continuum, have been studied over time. The characteristics of disintegrated communities include economic inadequacy, cultural confusion, wide-spread secularization, high frequency of broken homes, few and weak associations, few and weak leaders, few patterns of recreation, high frequency of interpersonal hostility, high frequency of crime and delinquency, and a weak and fragmented network of communication. The major hypothesis has been that mental illness is not randomly distributed and that a relationship obtains between conditions of sociocultural disintegration and a high prevalence of psychiatric disorder. Repeated epidemiological investigations have confirmed this (3). One might be moved to ask whether the apparent relationship between conditions of sociocultural disintegration and the high prevalence of psychiatric disorder can be conceptualized in terms which are meaningful for preventive mental-health programmes. But meaningful programmes are impossible without consideration of the total sociocultural context.

We have spoken of the importance of the physical environment in prevention and of adequate prenatal care and control of infection and injuries. In disintegrated communities, at least in Stirling County, not only mental, but also physical illnesses are highly prevalent. Medical services may or may not be available, but these communities are notorious for their failure to utilize such services.

Other discussants have said that the early years of personality development are important but that there are few guidelines for preventive activities. However, there is fairly widespread agreement that deprivation of significant relationships during critical developmental phases is potentially traumatic. In the disintegrated communities of Stirling County, the number of homes which are physically broken far exceeds the number in the integrated communities. Case studies add a dimension to such statistics and point up a striking characteristic – the ephemeral nature of human relationships in these communities. When poor mental and physical health abound, when intra- and inter-familial tensions are high, the chances for enduring human relationships are lowered. This finding is not unique to Stirling County. I think Oscar Lewis's "Culture of Poverty" (which he takes care to differentiate from poverty per se) is a very similar concept to that of sociocultural disintegration. In his books, *The Children of Sanchez* and *La Vida,* this same theme – the evanescence of human contact, because of tension, disease, and death – finds poignant expression.

Many studies seem to indicate that loss of a parent is related in a rather straightforward way to personality difficulties in later life. I would like to suggest, however, that even a factor such as this must be viewed within a sociocultural context. We have learned that the significance of an experience is determined by the meaning of that experience for the developing personality. The meaning of an experience is in turn conditioned by a set of sociocultural factors.

Leighton, Murphy, and their associates have studied an Eskimo village on Saint Lawrence Island. At one time, this was a well-integrated community. A disease epidemic, a world war, and dramatic social changes initiated a downward spiral and the bonds of social organization weakened and fragmented. In former days, when there was a true community on Saint Lawrence Island, a child who lost his parents was immediately adopted by another family within the village and blended with the other children of this family. In the later phases of community disintegration such a child became an "orphan" and was sent to an orphanage on the mainland, far from his birthplace.

Of the three aspects of prevention, the last, crisis intervention, seems most difficult to divorce from a sociocultural context. The very definition of a crisis depends upon such considerations. For example, consider the meaning a first pregnancy will have for a couple living in a rural, predominantly French-speaking village in what is essentially an extended family context and where the role of a woman is clearly and unambiguously defined as that of homemaker. Contrast this with a first pregnancy for a young, upwardly mobile couple, both of whom have professional aspirations and who live in the heart of the city, miles from either partner's family of origin. In the latter case, the situation might well be defined as a crisis; in the former, this is less likely.

Crises are apt to occur when guidelines for behaviour in novel situations are not available. In a well-functioning social system such guidelines are handed down as codes of behaviour and are used in coping with potentially stressful situations. Puberty rites are a well-known example of such culturally prescribed behavioural codes. In environments characterized by sociocultural disintegration, such behavioural prescriptions are few in number. As Oscar Lewis succinctly states the case: "One of the characteristics of the culture of poverty is the poverty of the culture." (6). It would seem that in such social environments the number of situations which will be defined as crises is greater than would be the case in integrated communities.

A basic tenet of crisis theory is that intervention by a community caretaker at a crucial time will lead to growth, rather than to disruption of the personality system. Even in this the disintegrated communities suffer; there not only seem to be more crises but fewer community caretakers. Church allegiances, for example, are weak. We cannot, in such circumstances, consider the ministry as a pool of preventive workers with the necessary prestige for such work. The same would apply to teachers and others with whom it is proposed that public health mental hygiene workers could profitably begin working.

Should all this inspire nothing but extreme gloom and pessimism or does it have any practical implications for preventive psychiatry? Can one go about changing the social system, and if so, will this have a beneficial effect on mental health? In 1949, Leighton and his colleagues selected a disintegrated community for intensive investigation (7). I use the term community, but this is probably a misnomer; it was actually a neighbourhood in which there was geographic proximity but in which there was so much indifference or mutual hostility that it could hardly be considered a community. There were no formal organizations or groups, work was regarded as a necessary evil to be avoided when possible, and church attendance, although espoused as good, was infrequent. The future was thought to be uncontrollable and most people felt that the best thing to do with a dollar was to spend it at once. A mental-health survey in 1952 revealed that the people suffered a high prevalence of psychiatric symptoms. The result was a vicious spiral in which lack of skills, damaging attitudes, and psychiatric disorder militated against satisfactory interactions with each other and also against effective interdigitation with the larger society. It could be added that the history of the region does not lend support to a "misery seeking each other out" hypothesis nor to an explanation of this community's existence as the result of genetic inferiority. Rather it seems that cultural isolation and a precipitous loss in the community's economic base initiated the trend toward disintegration.

In 1962 a resurvey revealed that change had taken place. The integration of the community as measured by social-science techniques had changed significantly and in an upward direction. Parallel with this change at a sociocultural level there were changes at the level of the individual. The prevalence rate of impairing psychiatric disorders was now considerably lower than it had been. Other communities which were disintegrated at the time of the original survey and remained so in 1962 showed no comparable shift in the prevalence of psychiatric disorder.

Time will not permit a discussion of the ways in which community development was fostered and brought about. This has been reported in other publications (7). The example is significant because it points up the high probability that community social organization is important for mental health. It would seem that if people can be helped to overcome some of their reluctance to act in concert by the gradual promotion of nonthreatening group activities, this may mobilize a powerful preventive and therapeutic agent. For one thing, social organization seems to bring in its wake not only improved community services but also an expansion of the cognitive map of individuals, so that they are able to utilize such services more effectively. We must remember that the provision of better medical services is important for prevention; promoting adequate utilization of such services is, however, equally important.

We might also guess, although this remains to be demonstrated, that increased community and family stability, and improved mental health of adults who are also parents will have favourable effects upon children. We would also speculate that in a socioculturally integrated environment, there will be better childhood socialization practices. Guidelines and role prescriptions, and symbols of adult success will be more clearly defined and easier to comprehend by developing personalities. Under such conditions we would expect a wider repertoire of coping behaviour, and hence, fewer situations defined as crises.

GENERAL VERSUS SPECIFIC APPROACHES:
INTEGRATION AND EPILOGUE

I hope I will not be accused of creating a straw man by raising the issue of specific versus general preventive procedures. There are some flesh and blood proponents of the specific approach who wave the finger of caution at psychiatry and public health. Consider, for example, the following quotation: ". . . I am most skeptical concerning the adequacy of our knowledge to develop significant techniques for treating social collectivities or for developing techniques on the community level that will really result in the reduction of mental disturbances in the community. It seems that such expectations are likely to move the psychiatrist still further from the more bona fide cases of mental illness in the community (9). Dr. Dunham goes on to say that the psychiatrist interested in such problems is guilty of the sin of the prodigal son: ". . . If he leaves psychiatry for another professional field, he divorces himself from the central task of psychiatry as a branch of medicine. He stops treating patients as patients. . . . I do not think we should kid ourselves that such movement constitutes the practice of psychiatry." Dr. Dunham raises again the issue of focus and chastises those whom he sees as rejecting the "bona fide cases" (which he seems to define as those which fit a medical model of disease). I hope this weary issue can be laid to rest at least for a time, in view of some of the considerations advanced earlier in this paper. As well as questioning the focus, Dunham once again confronts us with the appropriateness of techniques in his remarks about "treating social collectivities."

Such remonstrations notwithstanding, it would seem that "specific versus general procedures" is a meaningless issue. There is, no doubt, a great deal to be gained from working with relationships which involve short social distances and thus hew closer to a traditional clinical approach. Such programmes could reach more people by involving agencies already existing in communities. It should be noted, however, that in most mental-health programmes there is always a large residue of people who have come to be called "hard-core problems" and people with "inadequate motivation." These people are assigned such labels in fear and frustration when "specific" programmes fail to reach them.

Perhaps in such communities work over long social distances is the correct approach, at least at the beginning. Such work will involve closer co-ordination of efforts with community development workers, social scientists and economists. Thus the mental-health worker will find himself in increasing contact with what Harold Laswell has called the "policy sciences." From what we have learned in our research, success in fostering community integration may exert a preventive or at least an ameliorative effect.

An approach stressing short social distances is not incompatible with an approach which emphasizes the total system. It does seem that a necessary preliminary to the effective use of environmental resources, and this includes mental health facilities, is adequate community social organization. Therefore, all programmes must be viewed within a general context.

The general public-health literature is replete with reports of the failures of well-intentioned, well-organized preventive programmes which failed to consider the sociocultural context into which these programmes were being introduced (10).

For example, John and Elaine Cumming report their attempt to introduce an educational programme about psychiatry into Prairie Town, Saskatchewan. This well-intentioned effort had disastrous results. Their unfortunate experience resulted from a failure to recognize that the mental-health principles which were being taught were directly contradictory to a web of sentiments held by the community members. These sentiments in turn played a prominent part in the maintenance of the social system. In their report and in others, the same theme is reiterated – the importance of considering the sociocultural context (11). It would be lamentable indeed if behavioural science experts planning programmes of prevention, failed to take cognizance of such lessons from the past.

REFERENCES

1. See, e.g., LEMKAU, P. V. The epidemiological study of mental illness and mental health. *Amer. J. Psychiat.*, 1955, 3:801–8.
2. See LEIGHTON, A. H., D. C. LEIGHTON, and R. A. DANLEY. Validity in mental health surveys. J. Canad. psychiat. Assoc., 1966, 11:167–78.
3. LEIGHTON, D. C., J. S. HARDING, D. B. MACKLIN, A. M. MACMILLAN, and A. H. LEIGHTON. *The Character of Danger.* New York: Basic Books, 1963. Vol. III: *The Stirling County Study of Psychiatric Disorder and Sociocultural Environment.*
4. LEMKAU, P. V. *Mental Hygiene in Public Health.* New York: McGraw-Hill, 1955. Pp. 388–89.
5. LEIGHTON, A. H. *My Name is Legion: Foundations for Theory of Man in Relation to Culture.* New York: Basic Books, 1959. Vol. I: *The Stirling County Study of Psychiatric Disorder and Sociocultural Environment.* HUGHES, C. C., M-A TREMBLAY, R. N. RAPOPORT, and A. H. LEIGHTON. *People of Cove and Woodlot: Communities from the Viewpoint of Social Psychiatry.* New York: Basic Books, 1960. Vol. II: *The Stirling County Study of Psychiatric Disorder and Sociocultural Environment.*
6. LEWIS, OSCAR. *La Vida.* New York: Random House, 1966.
7. BEISER, M. Poverty, social disintegration and personality. *J. soc. Issues*, 1965, 1: 56–78.
8. For a more complete description of this study, see LEIGHTON, A. H. Poverty and social change, *Scient. American.* 1965, 212:21–27.
9. DUNHAM, H. WARREN. Community psychiatry: The latest therapeutic bandwagon. *Int. J. Psychiat.*, 1956, 11:564–65.
10. See PAUL, B. D. *Health, Culture, and Community.* New York: Russell Sage Foundation, 1955.
11. CUMMING, J. and E. CUMMING. Mental health education in a Canadian Community. In B. D. PAUL (9). Pp. 43–69.

6   Primary Prevention of Specific Disorders

Neurotic States / R. C. A. HUNTER, M.D.

I was asked to summarize the present state of our knowledge with regard to the etiology of the neuroses, etc. If these instructions are taken literally, it is clear that such a task is impossible within the compass of one paper. Therefore, I have been forced to take certain liberties with my terms of reference, and in order to orientate you, I would like to make these explicit. Firstly, I have gone over the literature in the areas of animal experimentation, child development, epidemiology, learning theory, and one or two other fields. The work on the influence of schools has been omitted, because Dr. Jack Griffin will be dealing with this more ably than I could. Work on transcultural psychiatry has also been neglected because this is, as yet, fragmentary and novel, and I have little confidence in my ability to present a judicious account of this important but somewhat unformed field. Secondly, those who are expert in any of the several fields of work with which I shall deal will note what they might well regard as significant omissions. Quite apart from the time factor, it must be made explicit that I have selected my material on the basis of what I have judged to be its relevance to clinical psychiatry and have made no attempt to be encyclopaedic, but rather to choose representative studies with which I happen to be familiar. It is regrettable but necessary that in the present state of our knowledge a presentation such as I am attempting must be preceded by a number of cautionary statements.

1. We cannot define neurosis with precision, and much of the work that has been done up to the present on the antecedents or early stages of psychiatric disturbance is relatively non-specific in terms of eventual outcome. By neurosis, in the present context, I intend to convey a definition which is negative in terms of severity (that is, not schizophrenia nor manic depressive psychosis), in terms of organic defect (not

mental retardation, nor epilepsy), but is inclusive of some behavioural problems, character deviations, sexual perversions, etc.

2. Extrapolation from the results of animal studies to human behaviour is fraught with uncertainty. As well as this general stricture, individual studies suffer from shortcomings specific to each experiment. However, by and large, animal studies possess the virtue of a much cleaner experimental design and their results should be more susceptible to replication than human studies.

3. In the relatively young but rapidly recruiting field of psychiatric epidemiological studies, there are the usual difficulties of case finding, case definition, heterogeneity of samples and criteria, and above all, the problems of control groups.

4. Child development studies as a group are either retrospective or anterospective. If they are the former, then, as Stella Chess has demonstrated, considerable retrospective falsification may occur, making the results somewhat less than secure (1). If they are anterospective they must cover long periods of time for adequate follow-up with the attendant difficulties of staff and subject mobility.

The above notations are not intended to be exhaustive catalogues of the inherent difficulties besetting each of these several forms of research: they are merely meant to remind you of the need for caution in the application of apparent knowledge gained from them. Having made this point explicit, I will not continue to repeat it throughout the remainder of the presentation since that would be both boring and irritating. As things stand now, today's "reliable study" may well be tomorrow's fallacy. Nevertheless, as Richmond and Lipton have so cogently pointed out apropos of preventive endeavour, "we need not apologize in clinical practice for acting on the basis of our best judgement in relationship to available data. Isolation for many infectious diseases was undertaken before we knew the specific infectious agent; fresh air and sunlight were considered desirable for infants before we knew of the specific effects of Vitamin D on bone growth" (2). What I propose to do may be likened to the flow of a river which, while it is full of pools, eddys, and whirls, some even flowing backwards against the main current, nevertheless pursues its over-all course in one direction. I fancy that I can indicate the general direction of the mainstream.

ANIMAL STUDIES

There are, by now, a large number of experiments with different types of animals the purpose of which it has been to demonstrate etiological factors leading to disorganized behaviour or impaired or altered task performance. You will note that I have avoided the use of the terms "animal neurosis" or "experimental animal neurosis." This is because it is very much open to debate whether animals can suffer "a neurosis" in the sense that we commonly apply the term to human beings. The animal experimenters have employed a variety of creatures, from the relatively simple to the relatively complex, in terms of brain structure, adaptational potential, and behavioural organization. Although, as students of man, we are apt to think of animal behaviour as relatively fixed and instinct dominated, it is well to recognize that some of the recent work, especially that of the ethologists, is exploding this myth and demonstrating that animal behaviour is considerably influenced by environmental and ecological conditions. Thus the behaviour of chimpanzees varies markedly in different environments. Also it is known that maturational patterns and rates differ considerably from species to species. These studies are gradually establishing behavioural pattern baselines against which to judge with greater reliability the significance of the behavioural response induced in the experimental animal.

Animal experiments have tended in the main to show that what is judged to be behavioural aberration or impaired functioning follows on a variety of circumstances. These include:

1. Physical or emotional insult delivered during intrauterine life, for example by dietary deficiencies, adrenaline and other hormonal injections, and other maternal stressors, including emotional ones. W. R. Thompson and others, using rats, have shown that high anxiety-drive levels in pregnant rats have resulted in offspring with sharply increased emotionality as measured by the open field test, defaecation etc. This correlation is very frequent but not invariable. The positive relationship has only been shown to hold quantitatively and not qualitatively (3). In addition there appears to be some relationship between teratologic agents, morphological abnormality, and behavioural aberration.

2. Interference with the normal developmental march of the animal, for example by surgical lesions, hormonal injections, dietary deficiencies, may later alter sexual, aggressive, and other behaviour.

3. Deprivation of various environmental stimuli or manipulation to the point of ambiguity may affect subsequent behavioural patterns. In this particular area a great many important contributions have been made, by such well-known workers as Lorenz, Tinbergen, Hebb, Harlow, and Ashley Montagu. In Pavlov's laboratory, dogs were conditioned to a circle which became the conditioned stimulus for food. The presen-

tation of an ellipse was not accompanied by feeding. As the ellipse was gradually made more circular and the discriminatory ability of the dog was overtaxed he struggled, howled, salivated, avoided feeding, and lost his ability to perform on other tests (4).

4. The blocking of various natural response satisfactions in the maturing animal may lead to the development of behaviour which is judged to be disordered. Thus, as Novakova has recently shown, if rats are weaned from the 15–30 days of post-natal life and tested at 8 and 12 months, it is found that those weaned earlier elaborated conditioned responses and memory traces more slowly, and the memory traces were less durable than in rats weaned at 30 days (5). The well-known work on REM deprivation also should be considered in this area, as should Masserman's demonstrations of cats who were deprived of expected satisfaction (6). At a more organic level a number of workers, including Langworthy, have shown that if infant animals are deprived of perceptual input there is not infrequently a residual organic defect. For instance, in Langworthy's experiments kittens were blindfolded from birth over one eye and it was observed that the blindfolded eye did not myelinize as well as the seeing eye did (2).

5. Manipulation of the social environment of animals may lead to disturbed behaviour as, for example, in the experiments on the pecking order of hens.

6. Experiments on over-stimulation, as in Liddell's "vigilance neurosis" and Brady's chimpanzees, all demonstrate that the application of a stressor over a sufficient period of time and under certain circumstances may lead to a variety of pathologic behavioural patterns ranging from disorganized behaviour in the dog and goat to ulceration of the G.I. tract in monkeys (7, 8).

7. Perhaps of utmost importance here is Horsley Gantt's observation that once autonomic nervous-system function has been conditioned to respond to given stimuli it is exceedingly resistant to change. Long after gross behaviour indicates that the animal is no longer responding with "anxiety" the autonomic nervous system continues in its state of arousal or imbalance.

Gantt also cites evidence from Bykov indicating that urinary secretion, thyroid function, metabolic changes, and even perhaps leucocytosis and immune reactions can be conditioned. He also mentions that a human being can be a more powerful stimulus for the experimental animal than food or faradic shock (9).

These findings, if taken in the aggregate, can be summarized in general terms as follows: indications exist from animal studies that interference with organic growth or development, deprivation of nurture or phase-specific developmental stimuli, learning experiences that overtax discriminatory ability, social manipulation or the deliberate evocation of fear responses may lead to subsequent aberrant functioning; some or all of which may have their human counterpart in the neurotic spectrum. Latent in these studies there is the strong suggestion that the timing of the influence under consideration is important, as in the ethologist's work, the weaning experiments, and the endocrine manipulation. The noxious influence can be lasting (chronic) or brief (acute). There is a tendency for an inverse relationship between severity and duration: the more severe the shorter the time over which it need act and vice versa. Since under natural circumstances organically defective or weakened animals would tend to perish, and since the species-specific mothering behaviour would provide that which is excluded or manipulated in the experiments, it follows that much of the resulting aberration can be subsumed under the heading of some degree of organic impairment with or without a defective mother-baby relationship.

CHILD DEVELOPMENT STUDIES

The difficulties in obtaining "hard" evidence in this area are to a considerable extent the result of ethical requirements which make it impossible to experiment with human babies and children. Nature and society, however, conspire to present the behavioural scientist with opportunities for observation, and even occasionally arrange an experiment of which advantage can be taken.

1. Studies by Pasamanick and his fellow workers on children born after the complications of pregnancy, especially uterine bleeding, toxaemia, and prematurity, have shown a significant association between these factors and cerebral palsy, epilepsy, mental deficiency, and, significant for our purposes here, behaviour disorders and reading difficulties. Tic was found more frequently in children born of complicated pregnancies but not in those born prematurely. Parenthetically, it may be well to note at this point for application later in this discussion, that the complications of pregnancy occur far more frequently in the socio-economically deprived sector of the population. It was found in Baltimore that the incidence of complications in the white upper economic fifth of the population was five per cent as against 14.6 per cent in the white lower fifth and 50.6 per cent in the non-white lower fifth (10).

2. The work on congenital-activity types in babies, begun by Louise

Despert, has undergone recent expansion. Stella Chess now describes primary or congenital "reaction patterns" which she feels are essentially primary since she has followed these children from 3/12 to 6 years (1). Dr. Dugal Campbell at Queen's University has been attempting to establish the range of normal behaviour for neonates and, using sophisticated objective measurements, has monitored the activity of 43 babies in the neonatal nursery. He has shown that a baby's "style" is constant from birth to day 10. By the fifth day of life, however, the baby's activity is markedly affected by the four-hourly feeding schedule. Just before feeding time activity reaches its maximum values. This is superimposed on the basic activity "style" of any given healthy baby. His studies of sucking and feeding in babies show that differences in sucking behaviour emerge in breast- and bottle-fed babies in the third and fourth days of life. For example, breast-fed babies, when they suck, do so significantly more slowly than do bottle-fed babies. One possible interpretation of this result is that even in the first few days of life babies can develop different habits of reaction based upon their feeding experience. The fact that differences in feeding experience are immediately effective in changing a baby's behaviour is shown by the fact that when they are pacified by the use of a rubber nipple, their heart-rate remains very variable; however, when they suck on their mother's nipple, or have glucose delivered to them through a rubber nipple, their heart-rate becomes slower and shows almost no moment-to-moment variability. This result indicates that the stimuli provided by feeding the baby have a much more powerful influence than a pacifier though in overt behaviour no difference can be detected (11). In this context, it will be remembered that Malmo and Shagass demonstrated a good many years ago that in neurotic adults indices of autonomic activity and muscle tension were a good deal more labile than in normals (12).

3. A philosophically related series of studies are those which have been carried out by Rose and his colleagues in Philadelphia into a breakdown in mothering related to various maternal or family problems, and illness or deformity in the child. This breakdown in mothering then re-acts on the child or children by inducing a degree of behavioural and physiological disorganization (13). Lussier from Montreal has published a beautiful account of the psychoanalysis of a congenitally stigmatized boy which adds depth to such studies (14).

4. Dollard and Miller offer a comprehensive and detailed explanation of neurotic behaviour in terms of learning theory as applied to the social matrix. This theory is anchored at some points in experimental work. The basic theory is based on the drive-cue-response-reward series of

instrumental learning theory in which learned inhibitions of drive reductions result in the accumulation of unsatisfied drive tensions. There is poor response-discrimination as a result, with inability to discriminate between nonpunishing and punishing situations. "The child is caught in a vicious circle in which learning results in maladaptive responses and these in turn, prevent the learning of more adaptive responses" (4). Henry Greenbaum uses learning as an organizer of the C-R sequence or link for the processes of imitation and identification and leans heavily on Miller and Dollard (15).

5. There are a series of studies of crisis situations which were initiated by Lindemann in 1944 (16) and have since stimulated other workers, notably Gerald Caplan, to work along similar lines. Time does not permit the thorough handling that this intriguing approach deserves, but I would like to spend a moment or two on its general philosophy and its significance. Following the observation that certain crisis periods in development must be met and overcome in normal childhood development, for example, grief, separation, birth of a sibling, it was observed that there also occurred exogenously imposed crises for example, financial disaster, parental illness, moving. Either of these types of crises occurring separately or simultaneously may lead to a "crisis reaction" in the child. Caplan describes it thus: "[if we consider] only the *intrapersonal* crisis in the child it appears that the fundamental manifestation of this is a period of behavioural disorganization and cognitive confusion; a temporary rise of psychophysiological tension, signs and symptoms of emotional upset, with a prominent appearance of anxiety, shame, guilt and depression; temporary lowering of effectiveness in dealing with tasks: an increased need for help from others; and an increased susceptibility to interpersonal influence." Caplan states that it is generally agreed that the exogenous or precipitating factor is a sudden loss or deprivation, or a developmental challenge which must possess some novelty in which past experience does not provide for the perception of a predictable course and/or solution (17). Similar observations were subjected to test by D. Wells Goodrich at NIMH in a carefully planned and well-recorded experiment. Two-and-a-half-year-old boys were taken from their homes and placed in a nursery-school observation setting. This represented a novel situation of separation for each child but with carefully selected and trained mother substitutes available in sufficient numbers in case of need. Goodrich and his team distinguished five reactions ranging from pleasurable mastery of the new situation, to panic, to a non-engagement pattern with emotional withdrawal and repetitive acts not directed at mastery (18). This line of work gives rise to some valuable generalizations and indicates further

fruitful areas for further work. It is clear that the conceptual framework on which it reposes is profoundly influenced by psychoanalytical observation and theory. The over-all concept of the "first time in the life of an individual that a thing happens," the circumstances under which it happens, the preparedness of the ego or state of maturity or strength of the ego at the time at which it happens, are all involved, as are the notions of mastery of excitement and the defences against anxiety. As far as I am aware, this work has not yet specified, with any reliability, how one can predict whether or not mastery will occur, or in what child, or what factors determine spontaneous irreversibility; or what the time relationships are between the duration of the distress reaction and chronicity. It seems a reasonable guess, however, that the state of the child at the moment of the trauma – which would subsume his past experience – dictates the meaning to him of the traumatic event. His preparedness for assistance makes its possible for effective and helpful environmental intervention to work. The matter is further complicated in that it seems that successful mastery is a growth-promoting and strengthening event and leads to further successful adaptational progress in some children.

6. A number of psychoanalytic workers, notably Sigmund Freud, Anna Freud, Melanie Klein, Eric Erikson and Hartmann, and Lowenstein and Kris have offered valuable constructs and conceptual schemata of personality development. The metapsychological view is well known but not always well understood, partly because of the shorthand terminology in which it is couched. Much of it, for example Miss Freud's, Mrs. Klein's, and Erikson's work spring from the direct observation of children and not merely from adult retrospective data. Apart from the well-known libido theory and the aggressive instincts with accompanying ideas on developmental phases, mediated by certain organs, culminating in the Oedipal phase, more recent developments involve ideas about ego growth and maturation as in Erikson's and Hartmann's, Lowenstein's and Kris's contributions. This work promises to provide lucrative bridging concepts and independent areas for research work such as some already mentioned. The modern psychoanalytical model has the advantage of sufficient breadth and flexibility to accept the available data but as yet lacks precision. It must be borne in mind, however, that no other conceptual scheme or model has come anywhere near to subsuming the obvious complexity of different durations, qualities, and strengths of insult reacting on a phase-dominated, experience-modified, flexibly adaptable organism with a repertoire of coping mechanisms and evolving adaptational results that occupy a spectrum from health to illness. It is to be expected that as opportunities for the longitudinal

psychoanalytic study of children increase, the method will make more definitive contributions. An example of this is Ilse Hellman's twenty-year follow-up study of a two-year-and-eight-month-old child who was left at the Hampstead Nursery, without preparation, by her mother. In this study it is notable that relatively little damage resulted from this trauma as judged by her twenty-three-year-old adjustment. This was attributed to the good relationship to the mother prior to separation, the adequacy of the available mother substitutes, and the competence of the environmental therapeutic intervention when necessary. This paper offers a fascinating and rich insight into the evolution of the coping mechanisms which Jane used in order to deal with her problems, and traces their contribution to her adult character formation (19).

EPIDEMIOLOGICAL STUDIES

This is a most difficult field in which to provide a succinct and yet reasonably accurate survey of the present state of knowledge. This is due in large part to the inherent difficulties of this type of research, some of which I have already mentioned, and which result in contradictory or even irreconcilable findings. It is not through mere laziness, therefore, that I shall begin by drawing heavily on "The Analysis of Field Studies of Psychological Disorder" by Dohrenwend and Dohrenwend in the *Journal of Abnormal Psychology* in 1965. These authors critically summarize the methodology and results of some thirty epidemiological studies that have been published over the past forty-five years or so. I shall skimp, perhaps unjustly, their own hobby horse of stressor-induced pathology because many aspects of this have been dealt with under the heading of "crisis reaction" earlier, and content myself with pointing out that when all these studies are analyzed comparatively the only finding which can claim substantial majority agreement is that there is an association between low socio-economic status and a high rate of judged psychopathology. They also feel, as I have indicated above, that the studies reveal the presence of much transient stressor-induced symptomatology which is defined as maladaptive, inversely with social class, and that more stresses occur in lower social classes. It is necessary, however, to remind ourselves at this juncture of Pasamanick's finding that the complications of pregnancy in prematurity are positively associated with lower social class, and that they are also positively associated with brain damage and its statistical sequelae.

I have omitted reference to the work by Bowlby, Robertson, and others on maternal separation and deprivation, as well as that of Spitz and Benjamin and others on hospitalism and institutionalization until this point because of the attempts by epidemiological methods to verify the original hypotheses. It will be remembered that a number of workers, notably Bowlby, advanced the hypothesis that loss of, or separation from, the mother disposes the affected small child to "mourning processes (which) habitually take a course that in older children and adults is regarded as pathological" (20). This is actually a particularization of Freud's earlier observation that the child is vulnerable and susceptible to anxiety about loss of many kinds, including parts of his own body, as well as external objects, or love, etc. It was not long before the sequelae of maternal loss or deprivation were extended to include other such clinical syndromes as delinquency, impulsivity, anhedonic states, and emotional or cognitive deficits. Although these views made an instant appeal to psychodynamically oriented psychiatrists and many child psychiatrists, it is striking that the epidemiological (usual retrospective) attempts to confirm these opinions by study of, for example, depressed populations, have been equivocal. In fact, there are as many studies which have failed to demonstrate a relationship between early object loss and depression, as there are those that have. I would think it is fairly safe at the present time to accept a positive but not invariable relationship between childhood bereavement and delinquency, behaviour disorder and/or reduction of cognitive function, and emotional coldness. I refer here to the papers by Brown, and Brown and Epps, in October 1966 (21, 22). The relationship to depression has yet to be demonstrated in epidemiological studies with satisfactory reliability. For instance, Alistair Munro finds none (23) and Constance Dennehy a few months later, in the same journal, finds a definite positive correlation (24). I myself feel that the point made by Ian Gregory (25) and others, including Dennehy, that much of the conflict of results is due to unsatisfactory control groups, is of crucial importance. Another factor which has not been satisfactorily taken into account, is that of spontaneous recovery occurring during the interval that is interposed between the original loss or separation and the time at which the study is carried out. Also, Winnicott has directed attention to the capacity of any individual child to tolerate aloneness and loneliness (26). The work on the problematical increase of emotional disorders among adopted children or orphans contributes little or nothing at the present time, in view of Kirk's recent conclusion in reference to adoption studies that "data of such uneven quality should not be used at all as a basis for findings" (27). The literature on stress reaction amongst soldiers need not be reviewed here. Suffice it to say that disability of sufficient severity to interfere with functioning have frequently been reported. It is of note that implicit in this literature is the observation that the inability to escape or avoid stressors seem particularly potent factors in causing the breakdown.

Mental epidemics, especially epidemics of hysteria, have been frequently reported, especially in the older literature. These tend to occur in populations under repressive conditions, for example, in girls' schools, and show marked elements of secondary gain or advantage (28). This later component has been inculpated by the learning theorists in the etiology and especially the perpetuation of neurotic symptoms.

Now, bearing in mind Richmond's point, of acting on our best judgment and in relationship to available data, we may attempt a summarizing statement with regard to the etiology of what we have defined as the neurosis.

1. Genetic factors, and constitutional factors such as prematurity, dietary deficiencies, toxemias of pregnancy, and uterine bleeding, may inflict minor degrees of brain damage, sometimes undetectable by available techniques, that lead to impaired reserves and adaptational potential.

2. With a given constitution, a child must proceed through maturational processes, which are, to some extent, genetically, phasically, determined in that the maturing organism has to complete certain tasks within certain time periods for growth to occur.

3. Disturbances can occur in this maturational march by virtue of a sudden, severe, brief trauma, or long-lasting, perhaps not so severe, insult.

4. These traumata or insults may be exogenous (social, familial, parental, etc.) or endogenous (metabolic, infectious, perceptual, etc.) and these can overlap in several ways.

5. Traumata or insults occurring during periods of intrapersonal phasic vulnerability are apt to be more disorganizing than otherwise.

6. The growing organism is especially vulnerable to deprivations or deficiencies; that is losses, or threats of losses, ranging from the physical to the emotional to the perceptual.

7. Such deprivations or deficiencies are more commonly encountered in the lower socio-economic strata of society.

8. The child responds to its perception of trauma or insult by attempts at mastery or restitution, according to its past experience, constitutional endowment, and genetically determined maturational phase.

9. Successful mastery is strengthening, unsuccessful mastery leads to a variety of less successful adaptational behaviours and is weakening and predisposing to subsequent mental illness.

10. Adaptational attempts may last from hours or days to weeks or months or may become fixed or chronic. Advantages may accrue to unsuccessful adaptational patterns, which will tend to reinforce and perpetuate them.

11. Accessibility to outside help is maximal during the phase of acute disorganization, and minimal during chronic adjustments.

12. Since successful mastery is advantageous, helpful intervention at the point of failing might be most effective.

13. Adults under stress may show similar patterns and run similar courses to children, depending upon past experience, the perception of the stressor, and feasibility of escape, and their constitutional endowment.

14. Once autonomic response patterns have become established they are markedly resistant to change or influence, except perhaps by drugs.

W. R. Thompson of Queen's University, who is making as determined an attempt as anyone, to establish a scientific developmental basis for personality, puts the general proposition in this way.

Firstly, the horizontal slice we take of the individual and call adult personality has a stratification that relates to different stages of development; *secondly,* the occurrence of such stages and the process of development itself are dependent on having a genotype; and *thirdly,* what happens during any one of these stages is determined by (a) what has happened during some previous stage and (b) the particular genes having an action that is timed to the particular developmental stage and (c) the environment occupied by the organism during this stage. (29)

REFERENCES

1. CHESS, S. A longitudinal study of children with resulting anterospective data. In J. H. MERIN (ed.). *The Etiology of the Neuroses.* New York: Science and Behaviour Books, Inc., 1966. Pp. 82–3.
2. RICHMOND, J. B. and E. L. LIPTON. Studies on mental health of children with specific implications for pediatricians. In G. CAPLAN (ed.). (17). P. 98.
3. THOMPSON, W. R., J. WATSON, and W. R. CHARLESWORTH. The effects of prenatal maternal stress on offspring behaviour in rats. *Psychol. monogr.,* 1963, 76, No. 38.
4. ROSEN, E. and I. GREGORY. *Abnormal Psychology.* Philadelphia: Saunders, 1966. P. 131.
5. NOVAKOVA, V. Weaning of young rats: Effect of time on behaviour. *Science,* 1966, 151:3709.
6. MASSERMAN, J. H. *Principles of Dynamic Psychiatry* (2nd ed.). Philadelphia: Saunders, 1961. Pp. 130 *et seq.*
7. LIDDELL, H. The role of vigilance in the development of animal neuroses. In P. H. HOCH and J. ZUBIN. *Anxiety.* New York: Grune and Stratton, 1950. Pp. 194–95.
8. BRADY, J. V. Ulcers in "executive" monkeys. *Scient. Amer.,* 1958, 199: 95–100.
9. GANTT, W. H. Antonomic conditioning. In J. WOLPE *et al.* (Eds.). *The Conditioning Therapics.* New York: Holt, Rinehart and Winston, 1964. Pp. 115–26.
10. PASAMANICK, B. and H. KNOBLOCH. Epidemiologic studies on the complications of pregnancy and the birth process. In G. CAPLAN (ed.). (17). Pp. 74–91.
11. CAMPBELL, D. Ms. in preparation.

12. MALMO, R. B. and C. SHAGASS. Physiologic study of symptom mechanisms in psychiatric patients under stress. *Psychosom. Med.*, 1949, 11.
13. ROSE, J. A. The prevention of mothering breakdown associated with physical abnormalities of the infant. In G. CAPLAN (ed.). (17). Pp. 265–82.
14. LUSSIER, A. The analysis of a boy with a congenital deformity. *Psychoan. study of the Child*, 15:430–53. 1960,
15. GREENBAUM, H. Imitation and identification in learning behaviour. In J. H. MERIN (ed.). *The Etiology of the Neuroses.* New York: Science and Behavior Books, Inc., 1966. Pp. 69–79.
16. LINDEMANN, E. Symptomatology and management of acute grief. *Amer. J. Psychiat.*, 1944, 101:141.
17. CAPLAN, G. (ed.). *Prevention of Mental Disorders in Children.* New York: Basic Books, Inc., 1961.
18. GOODRICH, D. W. Possibilities for preventive intervention during initial personality formation. In G. CAPLAN (ed.). (17). Pp. 255–59.
19. HELLMAN, I. Hampstead Nursery follow-up studies: Sudden separation and its effect followed over twenty years. *Psychoan. study of the Child*, 1962, 17:159–74.
20. BOWLBY, J. Childhood bereavement and psychiatric illness. In D. RICHTER *et al.* (Eds.). *Aspects of Psychiatric Research.* London: Oxford University Press, 1962.
21. BROWN, F. Childhood bereavement and subsequent psychiatric disorder. *Brit. J. Psychiat.*, 1966, 112:1035–41.
22. BROWN, F. and P. EPPS. Childhood bereavement and subsequent crime. *Brit. J. Psychiat.*, 1966, 112:1043–48.
23. MUNRO, A. Parental deprivation in depressive patients. *Brit. J. Psychiat.*, 1966, 112:443–57.
24. DENNEHY, C. Childhood bereavement and psychiatric illness. *Brit. J. Psychiat.*, 1966, 112:1049–69.
25. GREGORY, IAN. Retrospective data concerning childhood loss of a parent. *Arch. gen. Psychiat.*, 1966, 15:354–61.
26. WINNICOTT, D. W. The capacity to be alone. *Int. J. Psycho-anal.*, 1958, 39:1–5.
27. KIRK, H. D., K. JONASSOHN, and A. D. FISH. Are adopted children vulnerable to stress? *Arch. gen. Psychiat.*, 1966, 14:291–98.
28. TAYLOR, F. K. and R. C. A. HUNTER. Observations of a hysterical epidemic in a hospital ward. *Psychiat. Quart.*, 1958, 32:821–39.
29. THOMPSON, W. R. Personal communication.

Suicide / JOHN A. RASSELL, M.B.

Suicide appears to be the most personal action an individual can take, yet social relationships play an important part in its causation, and it has a profound social impact. While it seems to aim solely at destroying the self, it is also an act of aggression against others. The study of suicide illustrates that human action, however personal, is also interaction with other people, and that the individual cannot be understood in isolation from his social matrix. (17)

In recent years the annual deaths from suicide have been approximately

18,000 in the United States and 5,500 in Great Britain. These figures constitute a suicide rate of 10–11 per 100,000 of the general population. Non-fatal suicide acts, that is, suicidal attempts, have been estimated to be 6 to 8 times as numerous as suicides. Neither the triumphs of scientific medicine nor the rise in the standard of living have curbed the loss of life through suicide. They have, on the contrary, tended to increase it.

It is the purpose of this paper to present some facts and views about suicide and suicide attempts, as it is felt that this is a preventable condition. Indeed, Dublin (3) has stated that there is massive data on this problem, which suggests a field of public-health activity that has too long been allowed to lie fallow.

Suicide remains in a large sense one of the taboo topics of our society. Not only does suicide arouse profound and negative feelings in most people – much more so than other forms of death – but, because of the stigma cast upon the victim and his family, accurate data concerning the phenomenon have been difficult to gather. On a cultural level, these negative feelings encompass death in all its forms, but it is particularly true of death by one's own hand. As has been pointed out many times, each of us, consciously or unconsciously, is imbued with a personal feeling of immortality; in the social psychological area, neglect of this topic has occurred because scientists have been reluctant to intrude upon grief. Relatives and close friends of the suicide victim – many of whom could have done something to avert the tragedy, had they only recognized the warning signs – have made the research task difficult, and in many cases impossible.

There has also been the reaction of the scientists themselves – they too are susceptible to the anxiety surrounding death, and perhaps they too are protecting themselves from anxieties which are heightened by such activities as suicide research. On a technical and methodological level, the neglect of research has been related to a number of factors. The difficulty of determining the actual number of suicides, the absence of a system of reporting, and the difficulty in assessing the number of suicide attempts. Furthermore, much of the neglect in studying suicidal behaviour derives from the existence of contradictory theoretical explanations of the phenomenon. The sociologists find the theoretical-construct views of the psychoanalyst to be somewhat mystical – constructs such as a death wish, destruction of internalized super-ego, expiation of guilt, and so forth. The psychoanalytically oriented investigator, on the other hand, is equally confused by constructs such as state of integration, social system, and those theoretical orientations which do not include the individual as an individual, but rather consider the social system as the entity of investigation. A rapprochement between these two orientations may aid in overcoming the inertia in the area. The crucial problem is one of isolating the relevant social variables as they interact with the individual, including his conscious and unconscious wishes and desires (6). Progress is, however, being made, and I hope to illustrate some of the progress in this paper.

DEFINITIONS AND TYPES

Most investigators define successful or committed suicide as a violent, self-inflicted, destructive action, resulting in death. Attempted suicide is usually defined similarly, except that there is no fatal termination; but, as Stengel (16) has pointed out, the action must have a "self destructive intention, however vague and ambiguous." The suicidal gesture is similar, except that persons performing such an action neither intend to end life, nor expect to die as a result of their action, although the action is performed in the manner that other persons might interpret as suicidal in purpose. In suicidal threats the intention is expressed, but no relevant action is performed; and in suicidal ideation the person thinks, or talks, or writes about suicide without expressing any definite intent or performing any relevant action. Actually, all medical-legal definitions of "suicide" or "attempted suicide" do include the concept that the person played a major role in bringing about, or trying to bring about, his own demise, and that the conscious intention in his behaviour was to die. However, increasing evidence indicates that successful suicide and unsuccessful suicidal attempts represent two different kinds of acts, performed in different ways by different groups of people, although there is some overlapping. For example, successful suicides are more common among older people, males, and single, divorced, or widowed persons; reported unsuccessful suicidal attempts are more likely to occur among younger people, females, and the married population.

SOME ETIOLOGICAL APPROACHES

There have been many etiological approaches to suicide; a few will be briefly mentioned. Durkheim (4), as one of the earliest investigators, concluded that the common fact in all suicide patterns was the increasing alienation between the person and a social group to which he belonged. Other etiological studies have provided important information in relation to society. Cavan (2) related the suicide rates in urban districts of Chicago to the degree of social disorganization in those areas. Gruhle

(21) demonstrated how suicide rates vary with social and cultural variations in different geographical sections of Germany before World War II. Sainsbury (12), in a study of suicide in London, found that measures of social isolation correlated significantly with suicide rates. Yap's (22) report on suicide in Hong Kong also indicated the importance of the social matrix, noting especially high rates among immigrants from rural areas.

Freud (7) emphasized that melancholy and subsequent suicide often are a result of aggression directed at least partially toward an introjected love object, that is, a love object with whom the subject previously identified himself. He (8) later established suicide as the extreme manifestation of the active component of the death instinct directed against the self.

Menninger (9) made his well-known statement that the true suicide must expect to kill, be killed, and die, and discussed "partial" or "chronic" tendencies to self-destruction. Menninger saw suicide in any form as the result of the struggle between Thanatos and Eros, with the former winning.

It is apparent, however, that successful suicide is not simply an exaggerated or completed form of attempted suicide; formulation of dynamic theories about successful suicide by extrapolation from what has been learned in clinical studies of patients who have attempted suicide is hardly justified. In Stengel's and Cook's (19) extensive investigations, attempted suicide was studied as a meaningful and momentous event in the person's life, with special consideration of its effects on the social environment. Their chief conclusions were: (1) that the suicidal attempt is a phenomenon different from successful suicide, one that should be studied as a behaviour pattern of its own; (2) that an appeal to the human environment is a primary function of a suicidal attempt; (3) that the suicidal attempt has a variety of social effects, especially on interpersonal relations, which may determine the eventual result of the attempt. Indeed, Stengel and Cook have declared that in our society every suicidal warning or attempt has an appeal function, whatever the mental state in which it is made. Indeed, it would appear that in most true suicidal attempts, there is also discernible an effect of hidden or overt appeal to society, a "cry for help." The attempts are causally related to difficulties with interpersonal relationships and the social environment, and most attempters manage to maintain some contact with other persons, so that the call for help may be recognized. Both Stengel and Cook in their studies, and later Farberow and Schneidman (5), have demonstrated that such an appeal is inherent in most true suicidal attempts, irrespective of the mental state and the personality of the attempter. Evoking some change in the social situation, through the responses of an individual or groups to this conscious or unconscious appeal for help, is, then, one of the primary functions of such attempts.

EPIDEMIOLOGY

Successful suicide, or the more serious attempts, are most likely to occur among older persons, males, divorced, single, or married persons without children, persons isolated socially, persons with one or more close relatives dead, or who have a history of suicide in the immediate family, persons who have made prior suicidal attempts, persons who use shooting or hanging as the attempted or considered method, persons who attribute the act to "concern about ill health," and persons suffering from affective psychoses, schizophrenic reactions, delirious states, chronic brain syndromes, or chronic alcoholism, or persons who appear clinically depressed regardless of diagnosis. In the United States the rate has remained fairly constant since World War II, at between 10 and 11 per 100,000. Many countries have higher suicide rates than the United States, especially Japan, Hungary, Austria, Denmark, Switzerland, and Germany. In striking contrast, suicide rates for Ireland and Spain are extremely low, as are those in several South American countries. In the United States the suicide rate among adolescents is only 3.6/100,000, but the successive increment in each succeeding age group imposes a maximum rate of 27.9/100,000 by the age period of 75 to 84. In the younger age groups the rates for males are about 3 times those for females, but the over-all ratio is 10 to 1 or more. The rate for foreign-born American men is significantly higher than for the native born, the Negro is far less likely to commit suicide than the white, and suicide has been more common in urban than in rural areas. There is a maximum incidence occurring in springtime and the early summer months. Rates do tend to decrease in times of prosperity and during war and increase during depression. Members of the lower socio-economic classes have lower suicide rates than do members of the upper socio-economic classes, except after the age of 65, when the rate for lower-class males is considerably higher than that for upper-class males (20).

Epidemiological patterns of attempted suicide are far more difficult to analyze than those of successful suicide, because reports of the rates of suicidal attempts represent only a fraction of the real incidence of all suicide attempts among the general population. Estimates of the real rate of suicide attempts is at least 6 or 7 times as great as that of successful suicide. However, certain facts are known about such unsuccessful attempts; they are more common among females than males, especially in the population group under 30 years of age. The percentage of successful attempts becomes greater with increased age. Attempted suicides among the young are the least successful.

The studies of Sainsbury (12), and Stengel and Cook (18) suggested that about 1/10 to 1/5 of all persons who commit suicide will have made one or more prior suicidal attempts.

RELATIONSHIPS TO CLINICAL ENTITIES

Suicide is most common among persons diagnosed as suffering from the affective psychotic disorders, but is not uncommon among schizophrenics, and unplanned suicides have resulted from patients' confused states in delirium. Robbin's group (11) in St. Louis studied 134 consecutive successful suicides, conducting systematic interviews with family, in-laws, friends, job associates, physicians, ministers, and others a short time after the suicidal act. Using careful and well-defined criteria for illness, the results indicated that 94 per cent of those committing successful suicide had been psychiatrically ill, with 68 per cent of the total group suffering from one of two disorders: manic-depressive depression or chronic alcoholism. These results should be compared with those in an earlier study of 109 patients who attempted suicide, in which Schmidt *et al.* (13) found that the psychiatric disorders represented could be classified into nine different diagnostic categories; no attempter was thought to be "normal" prior to the attempt. Thus, attempted suicide is probably a symptom associated with a large variety of clinical psychiatric disorders, whereas successful suicide (probably including the aborted successful suicidal attempt) is most likely to be associated with depressive disorder of psychotic proportions and chronic alcoholism, and probably, to a lesser degree, with schizophrenia and organic disorder.

PROPHYLAXIS AND PREVENTION

Suicide prevention agencies can reach only a small minority in need of help. There is, therefore, need for very basic suicide prophylaxis which begins at birth and even earlier. Its aim is to eliminate or reduce all factors which tend to increase the incidence of suicidal acts and to strengthen all roles which tend to reduce it. The preservation of the family, active membership in a religious community or some other social group, the fight against alcoholism, good mental and physical health, good medical services, full employment, are all powerful factors against suicide. Divorce of the parents, physical or mental illness, alcohol abuse, widowhood, make suicide more likely. Some desirable advances may indirectly lead to an increase in the suicide rate. The triumphs of scientific medicine have benefited mainly the younger age-group, and enabled more people to grow old and sick and thus more liable to suicide. Improvement of medical and social care for the old would make a notable impact on the suicide rate. Perhaps the fight against suicidal behaviour is only one of the aspects of a much bigger problem which is the drastic re-orientation of society to the social needs of its members. Improvement of the existing medical and social services can contribute towards this aim, but this is not enough. Social isolation cannot be treated by doctors alone, or remedied by experts in social science. What is needed is a mobilization of the latent resources for helping and healing in our society; such help can be given by lay organizations (17).

In an article entitled "Towards Preventing Suicide," Parnell and Skottowe (10), investigated four questions: (1) is there a sufficiently large proportion of actual suicides who have not received full medical and social help? (2) If so, what warning signs can be discerned? (3) Is there evidence that admission to a mental hospital is preventive, not only in the sense of immediate prevention, like constant observation, but also in the sense of reducing the prospect of future attempts? (4) What evidence is there of the frequency of particular diagnoses among those attempting or committing suicide, and that those showing warning signs could be persuaded to enter mental hospitals, if most of them were not so manifestly ill as to warrant making an order under a mental-treatment act?

They investigated 100 consecutive suicides, and found that the majority had not received medical care. Thirteen per cent had been in hospital in the year prior to suicide, 27 per cent had recently attended their doctors, but had not been admitted to hospital. They concluded that the warning signs, of which a change of mood with appearance of depression, worry, or hopelessness was the most common, were not being recognized.

In their investigation into the preventive effect of admission to hospital, they point out that in 1954 there were 51 suicides in mental hospitals out of a total of 5,043 among the general population. They felt that admission exercised a preventive effect since there is a relatively small number of suicides in mental hospitals, that a large number of patients who have made unsuccessful attempts at suicide are subsequently treated successfully in mental hospitals, and since only a small number (13 per cent) of actual suicides are persons previously treated in a mental hospital, it seems safe to conclude that admission does exercise the important preventive effect expected of it. This study also shows only a small number of patients showing disorders of thinking, the change so often regarded by the public as a sine qua non for admission to a mental hospital. Of those they studied approximately 70 per cent were depressed or anxious. They concluded that, being less impulsive than the schizophrenic, psychopaths, etc., these patients are more likely to co-operate with treatment, or accept hospitalization.

Therefore, they concluded that in 100 consecutive cases of suicide the majority, 53 per cent, had not received medical advice, and only 13 had been in a mental hospital in the year preceding death. Warning signs present in the majority were change of mood with depression prominent, and previous attempts had been made by 11 suicides; the dangers inherent in depression must be grasped more realistically, and there must be a wider awareness of the positive effects of treatment. When depression is recognized, leading questions about suicidal thoughts are necessary to gauge the risk.

In a similar study carried out by Capstick (1), in which he had reviewed the coroners' records for a five-year period (1951–1955) covering 881 suicides, he concluded that examination of these suicides suggests that the number could be reduced by medical means: (1) signs of emotional abnormality were commonly present for some time before death; (2) comparatively few had received psychiatric treatment; (3) signs of profound depression sometimes did not receive the urgent attention which would have been given to a medical or surgical emergency; (4) comparatively few of the large population "at risk" in mental hospitals later commit suicide.

It would therefore appear important that the early signs of mental illness be recognized, particularly the recognition of depression; that there be ready access to hospitals, and that there be an adequate follow-up of patients discharged from hospital. A programme of public-health education is necessary in order to remove the taboo, to educate the community to awareness of the early signs of depression, and to encourage involvement of the family, and "the significant other" in those patients who have attempted suicide.

The use of lay organizations, such as the Salvation Army and Alcoholics Anonymous, can be of tremendous assistance in reducing the incidence of suicide. A more specific example of this kind of organization is the Samaritans (17), founded in 1953 by the rector of a small church in London, England, who through the usual means of mass communication, let it be known that people in despair and tempted to suicide would receive help if they rang a phone number at any time of the day or night. The team, consisting of two priests and a psychiatric social worker, form the nucleus of an organization which attracts a growing number of helpers and clients. Branches organized on similar lines sprang up in many other towns and have spread to other countries. Membership is confined to the laity and ministers of the church, with doctors serving as consultants only.

Finally, the Los Angeles Suicide Prevention Centre, is perhaps an outstanding example, and can serve as a model for centres in other areas. The Centre was established in 1958 and has demonstrated over the past several years the feasibility of (1) preventing suicide; (2) discovering prodromal clues to suicide; (3) doing social research on this topic; (4) using active therapeutic techniques, often involving the "significant other"; (5) acting as a consultation service for established health agencies; (6) working with a chief medical examiner coroner, especially by the use of the "psychological autopsy" procedure; (7) having an around-the-clock service; (8) employing a truly multi-professional approach; (9) reconceptualizing some time-worn (and inadequate) concepts of suicide and death; (10) "unbooing" some unnecessary taboos; (11) showing the desirability of establishing regional training centres; (12) operating a specifically focussed suicide prevention centre (14, 15).

The Centre serves as a short-term emergency clinic. In two-thirds of the cases, telephone is the only means of communication; referred patients are seen in face-to-face interviews. Special techniques for working with a patient by telephone have been developed. If special treatment is required the patient is referred to a hospital. Frequently the "significant other person" over whom the conflict has arisen is involved in treatment. The Centre has a 24-hour service, the nights being covered by suitably selected and trained auxiliary personnel. These "clinical associates" are students from psychology, psychiatry, social work, and other related fields who receive some remuneration for the service they give. The Centre has also taken on the task of informing and educating the general public about the problems of suicide through articles in the daily press, in magazines, and through appearances on television and radio by the staff members.

Studies at this Centre have shown that most individuals who are acutely suicidal are so for only a relatively short period, and that even during the time they are suicidal they are extremely ambivalent about living and dying. If the techniques for identifying these individuals, before rash acts are taken, can be disseminated, and if there are agencies in the community that can throw resources in on the side of life and give the individual some temporary surcease or sanctuary, then after a short time most individuals can go on, voluntarily and willingly, to live useful lives.

In this paper, I have attempted to point out the extent of the problem of suicide, to discuss briefly some of the epidemiology and etiology, to review some of the recent work on the preventive aspects, and have, I hope, indicated that the incidence of suicide can be reduced by a vigorous public community-health programme.

REFERENCES

1. CAPSTICK, A. Recognition of emotional disturbances and the prevention of suicide. *Brit. Med. J.*, 1960, 1179.
2. CAVAN, R. S. *Suicide*. Chicago: University of Chicago Press, 1926.
3. DUBLIN, L. I. Suicide: A public health problem. *Amer. J. publ. Hlth*, 1965, 55:12.
4. DURKHEIM, E. *Le Suicide*. Glencoe, Ill.: The Free Press, 1950.
5. FARBEROW, N. and E. S. SCHNEIDMAN. *The Cry for Help*. New York: McGraw-Hill, 1961.
6. FELIX, R. H. Suicide: A neglected problem. *Amer. J. publ. Hlth*, 1965, 55:16.
7. FREUD, S. Mourning and melancholia (written 1917). *Collected Papers*. New York: Basic Books, 1959. Vol. IV, pp. 152–70.
8. ——— Beyond the pleasure principle (written 1920). *Standard Ed.* London: Hogarth, 1957. Vol. XVIII.
9. MENNINGER, KARL. *Man Against Himself*. New York: Harcourt, 1938.
10. PARNELL, W. W. and I. SKOTTOWE. Towards preventing suicide. *Lancet*, 1957, 1:206.
11. ROBINS, E., G. E. MURPHY, R. H. WILKINSON, S. GASSNER, and J. KAYES. Some clinical considerations in the prevention of suicide based on a study of 134 successful suicides. *Amer. J. publ. Hlth*, 1959, 49:888.
12. SAINSBURY, P. *Suicide in London: An Ecological Study*. New York: Basic Books, 1956.
13. SCHMIDT, E. H., P. O'NEAL, and E. ROBINS. Evaluation of suicide attempts as guide to therapy. *J. Amer. med. Assoc.*, 1954, 155:549.
14. SCHNEIDMAN, E. S. and N. L. FARBEROW. The Los Angeles suicidal prevention center: A demonstration of public health feasibilities. *Amer. J. publ. Hlth*, 1965, 55:1.
15. SCHNEIDMAN, E. S. Preventing suicide. *Amer. J. Nurs.*, 1965, 65:111.
16. STENGEL, E. Attempted suicide: Its management in the general hospital. *Lancet*, 1963, 233.
17. ——— *Suicide and Attempted Suicide*. Harmondsworth: Penguin Books, 1964.
18. STENGEL, E. and N. COOK. Recent research into suicide and attempted suicide. *J. forens. Med.*, 1954, 1:252.
19. ——— *Attempted Suicide: Its Social Significance and Effects*. New York: Basic Books, 1958.
20. WEISS, J. M. A. Suicide: An epidemiological analysis. *Psychiat. Quart.*, 1954, 28:225.
21. ——— In S. ARIETI (ed.). *American Handbook of Psychiatry*. New York: Basic Books, 1966. Vol. III.
22. YAP, P. *Suicide in Hong Kong*, London: Oxford Univer. Press, 1958.

Brain Damage and
Mental Retardation / BENJAMIN GOLDBERG, M.D.

The field of mental retardation has moved so rapidly, with a wealth of studies in various disciplines, that only a sketchy overview can be given at this time. It is perhaps fitting that this is one of the early presentations in this series of Hincks' lectures, since the model for prevention of this condition is clearer than for some of the other illnesses encountered by psychiatrists.

This paper will consist of a series of diagrams and schemata leading toward a programme of detection, diagnosis, and prevention. At times, I will focus on some items of special interest. Figure 1 presents a

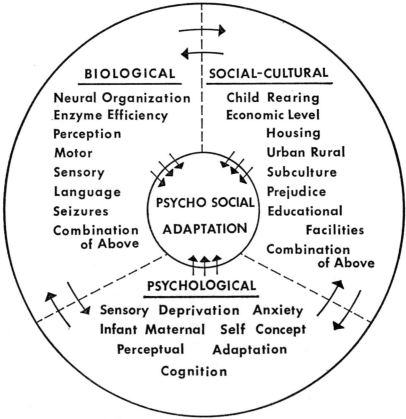

FIGURE 1. A Theoretical Model of Mental Retardation. From C. H. Carter, *Medical Aspects of Mental Retardation.* Courtesy of Charles C. Thomas, Publisher, Springfield, Illinois.

theoretical model of mental retardation (1). It will be noted that biological defects interrelate with sociocultural factors and psychological mechanisms in the over-all adaption of the developing human organism.

There are two popular definitions of mental retardation. The American Association of Mental Deficiency defines mental retardation as the *"subaverage general intellectual functioning* which originates during the *developmental period* and is associated with impairment in one or more of the following: 1. Maturation; 2. Learning; 3. Social Adjustment."

The World Health Organization defines *mental subnormality* as incomplete or insufficient development of the mental capacities, with: (a) *Mental Retardation,* lower functioning than would be expected from what is known of the intellectual capacities, and (b) *Mental Deficiency,* capacities diminished by pathological as opposed to environmental causes. I personally prefer the AAMD definition since it does not set up the mind-body dichotomy. It is also to be noted that intellectual testing must be performed to fulfil the criteria for this definition. In addition, the fact that the lower functioning must develop during the developmental period, differentiates this condition from the lower intellectual functioning which may occur in such periods as the senium when the condition would properly be referred to as dementia.

The systematic approach to the diagnosis of mental retardation, as practised at the Children's Psychiatric Research Institute in London, is presented in Table I. The list includes the concept of neuropsychological tests. This field is in its infancy but should become an important diagnostic tool, particularly for the child with specific learning deficits. The need for this has been mentioned earlier by Dr. Charles Roberts, in his papers.

TABLE I

DIAGNOSIS

1. Clinical History	6. Psychological Tests
2. Physical Examination	Psychometric
3. Neurological Examination	Projective
4. Mental State	Play
5. Laboratory Tests	Neuropsychological
	aphasia
	perception
	7. Educational Tests (mildly retarded)

In taking the history, special attention should be paid to areas which would indicate that the patient is a "high risk" candidate for mental retardation (2). The items which should be looked for in such a history are listed in Table II.

TABLE II*

HIGH RISK INFANT

Family History
  Presence of mutant genes   Previous defective sib
  C.N.S. disorders   Consanguinous marriage
  Low socio-economic group   Intrafamily conflict

Medical History of Mother
  Diabetes   Cardiovascular or renal disease
  Hypertension   Thyroid disease
  Radiation   Idiopathic thrombocytopoenic
                                              purpura

Previous Obstetrical History
  Toxaemia   Prolonged infertility
  Recent miscarriage   Size of infants
  High parity
  "Continuum of reproductive failure"

Present Pregnancy
  Maternal age < 18 or > 38   Radiations
  Multiple births   Anaesthesia
  Polyhydramnios   Rubella
  Pyelonephritis   Diabetes
  Out-of-wedlock pregnancy   Blood group incompatibility
  Oligohydramnios   Toxaemia

Labour and Delivery
  Absence of pre-natal care   Precipitate, prolonged or complicated
  Prematurity   labour
  Post-maturity   Low Apgar score—5 minute
  Dysmaturity

Placenta
  Massive infarction   Placentitis

Neonatal
  Single umbilical artery   Convulsions
  Jaundice   Congenital defects
  Head size   Size cf. gestation
  Infection   Severe dehydration
  Hypoxia

---

*Adopted from proceedings of the White House Conference on Mental Retardation 1963.

In looking at the factors listed under "previous obstetrical history" I would comment that there is increasing evidence for the support of Pasamanick's concept of a "continuum of reproductive failure" in which one finds within a given family a history of infertility, then miscarriage, then stillbirth, then mental retardation, then neuropsychiatric disorder within the children of such mothers.

TABLE III

LABORATORY DIAGNOSIS

Blood	Other
routine blood count	Tuberculin
fasting blood sugar	C.S.F.
serum calcium	chromosome culture
serum phosphorus	buccal smear
N.P.N.	Rectal biopsy
P.B.I.	brain biopsy
serum phenylalanine	liver biopsy
r.b.c. galactose-1-phosphate	audiogram
	audio-EEG
	E.E.G. and Electromyogram
Urinalysis	*X-ray*
galactose	Skull
albumin	Skeletal bones
phenylpyruvic acid	Pelvis
aminoacids	Pneumoencephelogram
polysaccharides	Angiogram
virus culture	Ventriculogram

A summary of the laboratory procedures necessary to establish a diagnosis of mental retardation is presented in Table III. (3) Unfortunately at this time these procedures are too expensive to be considered for use in mass surveys such as are undertaken for tuberculosis or diabetes. Rectal biopsy is listed. The aim of a rectal biopsy is to obtain samples of Auerbach plexus for neuropathological examination.

At the Institute we have found that even after completion of this extensive evaluation the cause may still be unknown in approximately 20 per cent of the children seen.

I feel that there has been an undue focus on the inborn errors of metabolism. These conditions have been popularized in both lay and medical literature out of proportion to the actual incidence in the population. Part of this biochemical research furor stems from the preventability of Phenylketonuria. It should be pointed out that some PKU children grow up with normal intelligence without treatment. The PKU carrier rate, however, is high in that one out of a hundred of the population carries the gene in recessive form. There are only a few cases of the other amino acid disorders reported in the literature. Yet the discovery of each new metabolic error which affects brain function gives another chapter in the understanding of brain biochemistry. In Table IV some of the currently known metabolic errors are listed with the preventable metabolic errors italicized. (4)

The most important cause of mental retardation in terms of incidence

TABLE IV*

INBORN ERRORS OF METABOLISM

	AMINO ACID DISORDERS	
Phenylketonuria	phenylalanine	convulsions eczema
Maple syrup urine disease	valine leucine isoleucine	spasticity myoclonic seizures
Tyrosinosis	tyrosine	myasthenia gravis
Hyperprolinemia	proline	g.u. anomalies photogenic epilepsy
Histidinemia	histidine	delayed speech
Citrullinuria	citrulline	convulsions vomiting
Hyperglycinemia	glycine	ketosis neutropenia
Homocystinuria	methionine	seizures dislocated lenses thrombo-embolic
Oasthouse urine disease	valine leucine isoleucine methionine phenylalanine tyrosine	white hair oedema unpleasant urine odour
Hartnup disease	neutral a.a.	ataxia rash
Joseph's disease	proline glycine	convulsions
Arginosuccinicaciduria	arginosuccinic a.	convulsions friable hair ataxia
Cystathiouinuria	cystathianine	congenital abnormalities psychosis
	LIPID DISORDERS	
Gargoylism	chondroitin sulfate heparitin sulfate	dwarfism hepatosplenomegaly corneal caterects deafness
Gaucher's disease	kerasin	spasticity hepatosplenomegaly
Tay-Sachs disease	ganglioside	muscle weakness blindness early death

TABLE IV (*concluded*)

Niemann-Pick disease	sphingomyelin	hepatosplenomegaly deafness athetosis seizures

LOSS OF LIPID ("BRAIN ROT")

Metachromatic leukodystrophy ⎫ Krabbe's disease ⎬ Pelizaeus-Merzbacher disease ⎭		deafness blindness ataxia seizures

CARBOHYDRATE DISORDERS

Galactosemia	galactose amino acids	hypotonia cateracts hepatosplenomegaly vomiting
Fructosemia	Fructose	vomiting hepatomegaly anorexia
Pompe's disease	glycogenosis	hypotonic cardiomegaly seizures

*PHILIPS, IRVING (ed.). PREVENTION AND TREATMENT OF MENTAL RETARDATION. New York: Basic Books, 1966. STEVENS, H. A. and HEBER, RICK (eds.). MENTAL RETARDATION. Chicago: University of Chicago Press, 1964.

TABLE V

CHROMOSOME ABNORMALITIES

Autosomes

    Tri-somy 21 or Translocation 21 (Down's syndrome)
    Group IV and V Trisomy (D) and (E) syndrome
    Triploidy: 69 chromosomes

Sex Chromosomes

Turner's:	45	XO
Klinefelter's:	47	XXY
Triple X:	47	XXX
		XXXY
		XXYY: Aggression
		XXXX
		XXXXY

Mosaics	*Other*
XX/XXY	Deletions
XX/XO	Inversions
XO/XXX	Duplications
XO/XY	Fragments: ⎧ Child Psychosis ⎩ LSD

are those conditions associated with chromosome abnormalities. These are listed in Table v. Mongolism or Down's syndrome is the most frequent cause of congenital mental retardation. In our out-patient series this amounts to 8 per cent of our population. The proportion is considerably higher in a hospital school for mentally retarded children. The factors producing chromosome abnormalities are still unknown. A specific gene or virus or other agent or "maturational" factor may play a part in producing such an abnormality. In the case of translocation mongolism specific genetic counselling can be given to prevent another such child being born. In the case of the other chromosome abnormalities genetic counselling is not so easy.

The sex chromosome abnormalities hold particular fascination for psychiatrists and other fields outside of mental retardation. The group at Johns Hopkins University, under Money, have been particularly active in the work on intersex abnormalities. In addition, the recent discovery of the criminally aggressive potential of having an extra Y chromosome holds particular interest for psychoanalysis, forensic psychiatrists, and cytogeneticists. Dr. Sergovich, director of our cytogenetics laboratory, and the writer have also reported on the increased incidence of chromosome fragments in a group of autistic children (5).

TABLE VI

TERATOGENIC AGENTS

Radiation	*Drugs*
Virus	propylthiouracil
rubella	corticosteroids
herpes simplex	stilbestrol
coxsackie	tetracycline
cytomegalic inclusion	vitamin K
mumps?	folic acid antagonist
vaccinia?	aminopterin
	quinine
Other Maternal Infections	phisostigmine
toxoplasmosis	
syphilis	*Smoking*
serum hepatitis?	premature infants
malaria?	
bacilluria	*Attempted Abortion*
	Anoxia
Endocrine	cardiac disease
hypothyroidism	pulmonary disease
diabetes	
cortisone excess	*Toxaemia*
	Nutrition
	excess vitamins
	low protein

The suspected human teratogenic agents are listed in Table VI. I feel that there needs to be a much firmer epidemiological basis for verifying the cause-effect relationship of these agents to mental retardation. Recent research also appears to focus on the significance of the presence of pus in the urine of pregnant women. It would appear that certain renal conditions in pregnant women seem to be associated with mental retardation.

Although the most frequent causes of mental retardation in all parts of the world are cultural familial factors, I can only say that, in terms of prevention, improvement of total socio-economic factors in a given society appears to have the most powerful affect in reducing the number of individuals with mental retardation. This would imply that the physician has indeed an important role to play in his community and in his general society and not purely in the confines of his consultation rooms.

I should like to point out a particular group of children with mental retardation who were reported by Dr. Hinton, consultant neurologist to our Institute. These were mainly retarded children with a history of fever and convulsions. This was the most frequent finding in the post-natal causes of mental retardation of children examined at our Institute (6). No organism was found in the spinal fluid of these children.

TABLE VII

Organic Post-natal Etiology

Injury (battered child, car, crib)

Infection
  meningitis
  encephalitis
  ordinary diseases of childhood
  fever and convulsions (Hinton group)

Poisons
  lead
  arsenic
  coal tar derivatives

Cerebrovascular disease
  haemorrhage
  thrombosis

Anoxia

Neoplasm

Psychogenic Post-natal Etiology

Cultural familial (nature vs. nurture).
Deprivation (Spitz-Bowlby)
Psychosis

Obviously research as to the possible causes of retardation in this group of children would be most important (See Table VII).

Some of the more likely areas for preventive medical research in the field of mental retardation would appear to be: further genetic research; looking for newer and more incriminating teratogenic agents; more refined virus studies in children with convulsions; the perfection of immunological studies including searching for a possible anti-brain factor or factors within high-risk mothers; the effects of psychological stress;

TABLE VIII

Primary Prevention

1. Pre-natal care
2. Genetic counselling
3. Avoid adverse psychosocial factors
4. Surgical
   hydrocephaly
   craniostenosis??
5. Medical
   dietary

Secondary Prevention

Medical
    anticonvulsants   ? Glutamic acid
    psychotropic drugs   ? "Brain Polisher"
    endocrine replacement   ? D.N.A. injection

Psychological
    individual therapy
    group therapy
    family counselling
       emergency
       supportive
       directive

Educational
    day care
    special schools
    remedial tutor
    vocational training

Tertiary Prevention

Social
    Placement out of home
       foster care
       group care
       institution
       short term
       long term
    guidance
    guardianship
    public education

psychological research into motivational and learning deficits in very young infants and children.

Our present knowledge of the prevention of mental retardation might therefore be outlined as in Table VIII. Until the 1950s institutional care was the only approach to a retarded child. The voluntary associations at local, provincial, and national levels then took the initiative in encouraging research and treatment approaches. In the 1960s research into causation and rehabilitation has accelerated in Canada. By 1970, community programmes should be blossoming.

Where will Canada be in our second century of Confederation in regard to prevention? Will we be regarded as primitive, as underdeveloped, as developing, or as well-developed?

REFERENCES

1. GARRARD and RICHMOND. Mental retardation without biological manifestations. In C. H. CARTER, (Ed.).
   Medical Aspects of Mental Retardation, Springfield, Ill.: Charles C. Thomas, 1965.
2. Proceedings of White House conference on mental retardation, Washington, D.C., 1963.
3. KOCH, RICHARD. Diagnosis in infancy and early childhood. In I. PHILIPS, (Ed.). *Prevention and Treatment of Mental Retardation*, New York: Basic Books, 1966.
4. EFRAN, M. L., D. YOUNG, H. W. MOSER, and R. A. MACCREADY. A Simple chromatographic screening test for the detection of disorders of amino acid metabolism. *New England J. Medicin*, 1965, 270: 1378–83.
5. SERGOVICH, F. R. Cytogenetic practice in a mental retardation clinic. *Canad. Psychiat. Assoc. J.*, 1967, 12:35–52.
6. HINTON, G. G. Postnatal Organic Causes of Mental Retardation. *Canad. Med. Asosc. J.*, 1962, 87:501–507.

In Geriatric Psychiatry / V. A. KRAL, M.D.

The importance of primary prevention of the psychiatric disorders of the aged needs no discussion. The report of the White House Conference on Aging (1), the report of the Canadian Senate's Committee on Aging (2), and the proceedings of the Canadian Conference on Aging (3) deal with the many problems which the increasing number of aging people pose upon society, not the least of which is the increasing number of mentally sick aged people.

In keeping with the topic of this presentation, no attempt will be made to discuss the various theories of aging. Suffice it to say that recent research seems to indicate that aging is part of the normal life-cycle, essentially an intrinsic, genetically determined process, but favourably or, for the most part, unfavourably modified by environmental extrinsic factors. In this presentation, the term aging is used as Birren used it: "as the regular changes which occur in adult organisms as they advance in chronological age" (4).

Psychologically, the primary process of aging is a slowing down of sensorimotor speed. According to Birren (5), this is not limited to one sense modality or to a particular response but involves all operations and processes integrated by the central nervous system. "Slowness of behaviour with age" will eventually appear in any individual who lives long enough, independently of disease and a wide range of environmental circumstances. Longitudinal studies have shown that diminution of sensorimotor speed is not related to longevity but rather to the IQ of the individual.

Our own clinical studies have revealed that a frequent psychological characteristic of normal human aging is a certain type of memory dysfunction that we have termed the "benign" form of senescent forgetfulness and which is fundamentally different from the "malignant" type of senescent forgetfulness, as found in senile dementia and other organic conditions (6).

Psychological and clinical studies have demonstrated that neither the diminution of sensorimotor speed, nor the benign type of senescent forgetfulness are signs of mental illness. The aged individuals are, as Birren puts it, "able to do most, if not all of the things they did previously but not as quickly."

In other words, from the psychological and psychiatric point of view, old age is not a disease. The mental disorders observed in the aged are not a direct consequence of the process of cerebral aging but rather completely independent of, or only indirectly connected with it. Consequently, primary prevention in geriatric psychiatry does not mean prevention of the aging process. It means prevention of the mental disorders commonly found in the aged and it depends on our understanding of the etiological factors involved and, furthermore, on our ability to eliminate or at least modify the etiologically important factors.

Our first task, therefore, is a clinical one, namely, to take stock of what mental disorders actually occur in the older age-group and to study their natural history. The steadily increasing number of elderly patients seen by psychiatrists and also the greater interest which psychiatry now takes in the older age-group, shattered the old belief that all psychiatric conditions encountered in the aged are due to structural changes either of the nervous parenchyma itself as in senile dementia, or of the cerebrovascular tree as in arteriosclerotic psychosis. Clinical research in various centres has convincingly shown that the mental disorders of the senescent part of our population comprise a variety of nosological entities.

Roth studied a population of individuals, 60 years and over, hospitalized in a mental institution in Britain (7). He found that, out of 450 patients, 266 (59.3 per cent) were suffering from functional psychoses: 220 (49.1 per cent) of these from affective disorders and 46 (10.2 per cent) from late paraphrenia. Acute and subacute confusional states were found in 36 (8.5 per cent) cases and only the remaining 146 patients (32.2 per cent) were actually suffering from psychoses due to organic brain disease: 36 (8 per cent) had arteriosclerotic psychoses and 110 (24.2 per cent) were suffering from senile psychoses.

Six months after admission, 65 (59 per cent) of the 110 senile patients had died; 33 (30 per cent) were still in the hospital; and only 12 (11 per cent) were discharged. Of the 36 patients with arteriosclerotic psychoses, 12 (33 per cent) had died, 16 (46 per cent) were in-patients and 8 (23 per cent) were discharged. Of the 220 patients suffering from affective psychoses, on the other hand, 23 (10 per cent) had died, 83 (38 per cent) were in the hospital; and 114, which is more than 50 per cent, were discharged. As for the cases with late paraphrenia: 2 (4 per cent) were dead; 36 (79 per cent) were in the hospital; and 8 (17 per cent) were discharged. The patients suffering from acute confusion occupied a middle position between the organic and the functional groups. Two years after admission each disease had largely maintained its distinctive pattern of outcome. The only notable exception was that in the group of arteriosclerotic patients the percentage of deaths had climbed from 33 to 73 per cent, whereas in the senile patients it had reached 82 per cent. The group of confusional states, two years after admission, was evenly divided between the dead and the discharged.

Roth's study suggests that affective psychoses, late paraphrenia, and acute confusion are distinct from the two main causes of progressive dementia in old age: senile and arteriosclerotic psychoses. In addition, the study also provided some validity as to the distinction between these two dementing psychoses, although the clinical differentiation may be difficult in a given case.

Using the same criteria, we recently reviewed the material of the geriatric service of the Douglas Hospital in Montreal. Of 695 patients of both sexes, with a mean age of 75.3 years, 279 (40 per cent) were found to be suffering from functional psychoses, although on admission a diagnosis of psychosis with senile brain disease had been made for a great number of them (8).

Another study (9) undertaken by our group showed the following: Of 210 cases seen by the psychiatrists in a geriatric outpatient clinic, 19 (9 per cent) were found without psychiatric disorder on clinical psychiatric examination; 91 (43 per cent) were suffering from neurotic conditions; 41 (19.5 per cent) were found to have senile psychoses; 12 (5.7 per cent) arteriosclerotic psychoses; and 41 (19.5 per cent) functional psychoses. Among the latter, endogenous depressions of the manic-depressive and the involutional type prevailed. These were found in 34 of the 41 cases. Late paraphrenia was present in the remaining seven cases. It is interesting to note that the main difference between Roth's study which comprised the case material of a closed mental hospital and the clinical study just mentioned consists in the fact that in his material affective psychosis was the most frequent diagnosis, whereas, in our clinical material the main bulk of the cases consisted of neurotic reactions. The differences in the incidence of the organic disorders were surprisingly small.

In summarizing these studies, we arrive at the following conclusions: (1) In the senescent segment of our population there occur at least six kinds of mental disorders of numerical importance which differ as to symptomatology, course, and outcome. These are neurotic reactions, functional psychoses of the manic-depressive type, late paraphrenias, arteriosclerotic psychoses, senile psychoses, and acute confusional states. (2) The psychotic conditions caused by structural brain disease of the senile and arteriosclerotic type are numerically less important than previously assumed and amount only to approximately 25–30 per cent of the material. (3). Functional disorders of the affective type, particularly endogenous depressions, form a considerable part of the mental disorders of older patients in and outside mental hospitals. (4) Among the non-hospitalized old people, neurotic conditions form the most frequently encountered type of mental disorders.

Of the six nosological entities just mentioned there is only one about whose main causative factor we are fairly certain: that is the group of the neurotic reactions in later life which comprises the main bulk of the cases which psychiatrists see outside a mental hospital. The problems of these patients are primarily those of adjustment to the biological, psychological, and social facts of aging. Their histories reveal that they had difficulties in adjustment earlier in life in critical periods and in conflict situations. Now, with advancing age, they have to adjust to new and mostly unfavourable situations at a time in life when the capacity for adaptation weakens. The most important factors involved are the loss of prestige among family and friends, the loss of a life-long occupation (be it a job or housekeeping), decreased earning capacity, and frequently a drastically decreased income. This leads to increasing dependence on others at a time when the spouse or life-long friends are being lost.

The main dynamic factor in these neurotic conditions is anxiety – the aging person's anxiety about getting old, losing his role in society, and becoming isolated and rejected. There is also the anxiety of the younger members of society about their own future aging, which leads to a tendency on their part to separate themselves from the aging person, to close their eyes to his problems, and also to disregard the positive sides of aging: greater experience, better judgment, less emotional reactivity, and better control of some of the drives which motivate and govern the younger years in life.

This largely unconscious anxiety on the part of younger members of the community may be partly to blame for the fact that society has not been sufficiently prepared to deal with the socio-economic and socio-psychological consequences of the increased longevity of an increasing proportion of our citizens. Thus, a situation has developed which is damaging to many aging people and contributes to their increased psychiatric morbidity. This in turn increases the anxiety felt by younger citizens and leads to their rejection of the ailing aged. A vicious circle has been established which must be broken.

A change in this attitude and also the increasing number of aging people in the population will make them, ipso facto, a powerful force, and this should, in the future, help an aged person to deal with his own anxiety. With proper education in youth and adult years, he will learn to accept and adjust to aging. Society is beginning to realize its obligations to provide work for the aging within the limits of their ability. Studies of the good and bad effects of retirement are in progress in many centres and it is reasonable to hope that active measures will soon be taken to improve the situation of the aged.

The second disease entity for which we know something of the pathogenesis and etiology is the acute and subacute confusional states of the aged (10). These conditions develop in old people under the impact of various infections, toxic, traumatic, and other physical noxae, the common denominator of which is the acute stress they exert on the aging organism. Psychological stress, if severe enough, may also produce a confusional state. The stressor effect in these cases is unspecific. The stress acts on the patient at a time in life when his stress tolerance is declining. A condition which is harmless and easily tolerable for the healthy adult and the middle-aged person may become a danger to the mental health of the old person or may possibly even lead to death as shown in the figures of Roth's study. The immediate conclusion to be drawn from such observations is that acute stress of any kind should be avoided by the old person. Not only should the recommendations of physical hygiene and medicine strictly be observed, it is also necessary to protect the aged as far as possible from the socio-economic and socio-psychological stresses. This of course is the responsibility of the younger members of society, who also have to provide the necessary supervision and the frequently needed help.

Our knowledge of the etiology of the endogenous affective disorders of the manic-depressive and the involutional type is limited and the same holds true for schizophrenia, to which the cases of late paraphrenia apparently belong. We know that in both conditions genetic factors are of etiological importance. We also assume that in both diseases environmental factors such as stressful and conflictual situations may play a role, although the opinion of the various authors and schools vary as to the relative importance of these sets of factors. I should like to mention, however, that, while we are not in a position to recommend scientifically valid, preventive measures for manic-depressive and schizophrenic illness, psychiatry has developed effective means to treat the functional psychoses of the affective and schizophrenic type, even in later life, by psychopharmacological and other methods.

In discussing the two main groups of chronic organic diseases, we have to consider arteriosclerotic psychosis separately from senile psychosis, as the former involves primarily the vascular apparatus, the latter primarily the brain substance. Kallmann's studies of twins (11) and other genetic investigations (12) tend to demonstrate a hereditary factor as operative in the etiology of cerebral arteriosclerosis. Information is also accumulating indicating a metabolic disorder related to the fat and lipid metabolism, as an important pathophysiological factor in this disease (13). Psychiatric experience, on the other hand, seems to show that people already affected by arteriosclerotic brain disease are less tolerant to stress and may respond to acute stress by an aggravation of the already existing mental dysfunction or an acute confusional state or a stroke. Preventive measures would, therefore, have to include, in addition to proper dietary habits, the avoidance of acute stress in a manner similar to that mentioned above.

Our knowledge of the etiology of senile brain disease is also limited. Kallmann's investigations (14), as well as a recent study by Larsson, Sjoergen, and Jacobsen (15) seem to indicate that here, too, hereditary factors are operative. Rothschild (16), on the other hand, stresses the fact that the severity of the clinical picture in senile psychosis does not strictly parallel the severity of the gross and microscopic changes in the brain. Other factors, particularly acute stress suffered by the aged organism, may be of etiological importance. Kral's experiences in a concentration camp during the war (17) demonstrated that, whereas functional psychoses apparently did not increase in frequency as compared to peacetime conditions and neurotic conditions even improved, senile psychoses showed a considerable increase in frequency, most probably due to the stressful conditions in the camp.

It is not impossible, however, that stress endured in the past may also be of importance in the etiology of senile psychosis. Wolff found that people who had undergone stressful experiences for a prolonged period of time showed the same type of impairment of the highest integrative functions as did organically brain-damaged patients (18). Busse, who studied the EEG's of aged subjects showed that people of lower socio-economic status, who presumably had been exposed to more severe hardships, had a significantly higher percentage of dysrhythmic electroencephalograms as compared to subjects of the same age-group belonging to the upper social classes (19).

Observations such as these motivated our own research into the role of stress in the etiology of senile psychosis. The question of what effect stress endured in the past may have in this respect was investigated through studies of the residents of an old people's home. Their life histories, from birth to the present were investigated by social workers using questionnaires. All residents were also examined psychiatrically and neurologically and were tested by a battery of psychological tests. They were grouped on the basis of the clinical and psychological findings in two main groups: those who did not show signs of organic brain disease of the senile and arteriosclerotic type and those in whom clinical signs of either of these diseases were present. No differentiation between senile and arteriosclerotic brain disease was attempted for the purpose of this study.

Of the 112 residents (55 women and 57 men) with a mean age of 81, 63 (24 women and 39 men) did not show signs of organic brain disease, whereas 49 (31 women and 18 men) demonstrated such signs. Statistical analysis revealed that there was no significant difference in age between the residents with and without organic brain disease.

Inquiry into the life history of the subjects showed that organic brain damage was significantly less frequent in those subjects who showed good relationships to their parents, siblings, and friends in childhood and adult life. There was also a significant difference, in favour of the former group, in early emotional security and also in good adjustment to jobs. The same applied to marital adjustment and parental roles. The people without organic brain disease showed a significantly higher proportion of good adjustment to aging than did those with organic brain disease. There was, however, no significant difference between the groups in regard to the financial situation of the subjects nor was there, and this appeared surprising, any significant difference between those who had enjoyed good health most of their life, as opposed to those who had been frequently sick or sick for long periods of time. Many other factors which were studied and statistically analyzed were of no importance for the problem of whether the patient would develop organic brain disease in old age or not.

These studies led to the following conclusions: those subjects who experienced emotional insecurity in childhood developed organic brain disease in old age significantly more frequently than those whose childhood was emotionally secure; those subjects who later showed organic brain disease were significantly less adaptable in the face of stress throughout their total life situation. It was interesting to note that women particularly broke down in their ability to adapt to difficulties in their marital life and on such occasions had suffered both physical and mental diseases. It was also found that those subjects who had greater inner resources, particularly intellectual resources, were significantly more prevalent in the group without organic brain disease than in the group with such signs. We are therefore led to believe that early emotional security seems to be of importance for the future adaptability to stress and this, in turn, seems to have a significant bearing on the question of whether the person may or may not develop organic brain disease in old age (20).

As Comfort puts it, the aging organism shows: "a decline in resistance to random stresses," a view which is supported by clinical experience and laboratory experiments (21). Another line of our research was, therefore, designed to investigate the stress tolerance of patients suffering from senile psychosis as compared with other groups. For this purpose various types of stresses are being used and there are several forms of tests to assess their effect.

Our present studies seem to indicate that the adrenocortical response to stress is different in normal old people, in patients with senile dementia, and in chronologically old schizophrenics, thus lending support to the demand for a careful differential diagnosis of the mental disorders in old people. Furthermore, our investigations indicate that, psychologically, the patient with senile dementia does not react to stressful situations in the way that normal young and old people and old patients with functional psychoses do. Indeed, a psychological reaction of the patients with senile dementia to stressful situations may be missing, thus exposing them to great dangers in life (22).

The question now arises of whether we are able to increase the aging organism's resistance to stress. Experiments conducted in our laboratory over the past years seem to indicate two possible ways to achieve this end. One is to adapt the aging organism to stressful situations. Animal experiments conducted in our laboratory seem to indicate that adaptation to stress, although effective to a certain extent, is still less effective in the old animal than in the young ones (23).

Another possible method would be the use of certain biologically active substances. We have tried a number of such substances – thyroid extract, ACTH, cortisone, and others – but did not find them effective in the stress bio-assay which we developed on the basis of the previous studies. Other experiments concerned the effects of royal jelly. When royal jelly in a dosage of 0.001 ml is injected into old mice which had been gradually adapted to the stress of cold there is a significantly longer survival time in comparison with both unadapted old animals treated with royal jelly and adapted old animals which were not given the substance. But even then the survival time was significantly shorter than in younger animals (24). These and similar animal studies are still in progress. So far, however, our experiments tend to show that neither the adaptation to stress nor the application of biologically active substances does effectively increase the aging organism's resistance to stress.

SUMMARY

Our studies, both clinical and experimental, lead us to the following conclusions. The mental disorders found in the aging population are varied as to their nature, etiology, and course. One can define at least six numerically important kinds of mental disorders in the aged. Prevention should be based on the etiology of these disorders, which unfortunately is still largely unknown. Clinical experience tends to show that one of these disorders seems to be psychologically connected with aging: namely, the group of neurotic reactions of aged people. It is in this field that preventive measures mainly of a social and psychological nature could and should be started immediately, although the effect may become manifest only in future generations. Acute and chronic stress suffered in old age seems to be an important factor in the etiology of mental disorders of the aged. Indications are that patients suffering from various types of mental disorders in old age may react differently to acute stress both physically and psychologically. Above and beyond these findings it would appear that emotional security in childhood tends to increase an individual's ability to adjust to stressful situations in later life and thereby to protect him against their damaging effect in old age.

REFERENCES

1. White House conference on ageing. *Geriatrics*, 1961, 16:111–52.
2. Final Report of the Special Committee of the Senate on Aging. Ottawa, The Senate of Canada, 1966.
3. Proceedings, The Canadian Conference on Aging, Toronto 1966. Ottawa, Canadian Welfare Council, 1966.
4. BIRREN, J. E. Behavioral theories of aging. In N. W. SHOCK (Ed.). *Aging.* Publication No. 65, Amer. Assoc. f. the Advancement of Science, 1960.
5. ——— Neural basis of personal adjustment in aging. In *Age with a Future: Proceedings of the Sixth International Congress of Gerontology, Copenhagen 1963.* Copenhagen: Ejnar Munksgaard, 1964.
6. KRAL, V. A. Senescent forgetfulness: Benign and malignant, *Canad. med. assoc. J.*, 1962, 86:257–60.
7. ROTH, M. The natural history of mental disorder in old age. *J. Ment. Sci.*, 1955, 101:281–301.
8. KRAL, V. A., C. CAHN, and H. MUELLER. Senescent memory impairment and its relation to the general health of the aging individual. *J. Amer. Geriat. Soc.*, 1964, 2:101–13.
9. KRAL, V. A. and S. GOLD. Psychiatric findings in a geriatric outpatient clinic. *Canad. med. assoc. J.*, 1961, 84:588–90.
10. KRAL, V. A. Stress and mental disorders of the senium. *Med. serv. J. Canada*, 1962, 18:363–70.
11. KALLMANN, F. J. Genetic aspects of mental disorders in later life. In O. J. KAPLAN (Ed.). *Mental Disorders in Later Life* (2nd ed.). Stanford: Stanford Univ. Press, 1956.
12. GLASS, B. Anatomical and biochemical aspects of heredity in reference to atherosclerosis. In *Symposium on Atherosclerosis.* Publ. 338, National Academy of Sciences. Washington: Nat. Res. Council, 1954.
13. MOSES, C. *Atherosclerosis.* Philadelphia: Lea and Febiger, 1963.
14. KALLMANN, F. J. The genetics of mental illness. In S. ARIETTI (Ed.). *American Handbook of Psychiatry.* New York: Basic Books, 1959.
15. LARSSON, T., T. SJOERGEN, and G. JACOBSON. *Acta Psychiatr. Scand.*, 39 (Suppl. 167), 1963.
16. ROTHSCHILD, D. Senile psychoses and psychoses with cerebral arteriosclerosis. In O. J. KAPLAN (Ed.). *Mental Disorders in Later Life* (2nd ed.). Stanford: Stanford Univ. Press, 1956. Pp. 289–331.
17. KRAL, V. A. Psychiatric observations under severe chronic stress. *Amer. J. Psychiat.*, 1951, 108:185–92.

18. WOLFF, H. G., L. F. CHAPMAN, W. N. THETFORD, L. BERLIN, and T. C. GUTHRIE. Highest integrative functions in man during stress. In *The Brain and Human Behavior*. Baltimore: Williams and Wilkins, 1958.
19. BUSSE, E. W. Psychopathology. In J. E. BIRREN (Ed.). *Handbook of Aging and the Individual*, Chicago: Univ. of Chicago Press, 1959. Pp. 364–78.
20. KRAL, V. A. Recent research in prevention of mental disorders at later age levels. In R. H. OJEMANN (Ed.). *Recent Research Looking Toward Preventive Intervention: Proceed. of the Third Institute on Preventive Psychiatry*. Iowa, 1961.
21. COMFORT, A. *The Biology of Senescence*. New York: Holt, Rinehart and Winston, 1956.
22. KRAL, V. A., B. GRAD, F. CRAMER-AZIMA, and L. RUSSELL. Biologic, psychologic and sociologic studies in normal aged persons and patients with senile psychosis. *J. Amer. Geriat. Soc.*, 1964, 12:21–37.
23. GRAD, B. and V. A. KRAL. Adrenal cortical stress effects in senility: II. *Canad. Psychiat. Assoc. J.*, 1961, 6:66–74.
24. GRAD, B., V. A. KRAL, and J. BERENSON. Toxic and protective effects of royal jelly in normal and diseased mice. *Canad. J. Biochem. Physiol.*, 1961, 39:461–76.

Delinquency / A. LAMBERTI, M.D.

In recent years increasing attention has been given by educators to the restless, impulsive, easily distractible child who interfered with the learning process of his peers. Formerly, these children were tolerated and given social promotions to successive grades. This indifferent approach to this category of child has been altered by the recognition that certain unfavourable factors can foster the behavioural disorder pattern in a child. It has been known for years that children of parents in the low socio-economic group living in depressed housing areas were extremely prone to behavioural disorders. Developmental studies (2, 4) of these children have repeatedly shown that behavioural disorders can be the consequences of psychological deprivation in early childhood.

Behaviourally, the child has presented the picture of passivity, inability to form warm interpersonal relationships, with intellectual impoverishment and failure to develop adequate abstract concepts. Observations in a nursery-school setting in a skid-row area indicated developmental deviations could be found as early as two-and-a-half years of age (7). It was also noted that, although these children might appear to be somewhat precocious, they were actually unresponsive to stimuli which normally aroused eagerness in children – new displays in the nursery school – and were hyperalert to stimuli which the average child takes for granted – for example, these children continually scanned the room for the presence of the teacher without making any attempt to gain the teacher's attention. It was hypothesized that these children developed a pattern for coping with life at an early stage because they lived in a neighbourhood where strife, fights, quarrels, and slaps were common and where automotive traffic was heavy. The price paid for this pattern was a literalness and inability to shift freely to new experiences.

Recognition that most of these children will become developmental casualties has brought forward projects such as Headstart, Operation Bootstrap, and Catchup, to become operative at the pre-school level. These projects, functioning within a therapeutic day-nursery setting, offer such children graduated doses of socialization and familiarization experiences. The parents may in addition be encouraged to enter into group-work process or may have a home visitor assigned to them as part of the total programme. These children still require further assistance within a regular school setting in order to ensure that the gains made in the nursery school setting are not lost (10). The child who fails to integrate incoming stimuli from the external world into a meaningful message may present as a behavioural disorder in the classroom (3). Disciplinary attempts by the teacher may increase the child's difficulty in learning and produce a secondary emotional reaction. Educational treatment facilities within the school system have been developed to remedy the perceptual handicap.

At this juncture, one might state that behavioural disorders arising from psychologic deprivation may be prevented if the developmental deviation can be altered via the therapeutic day nursery and further help given within the early school years. The recognition and treatment of an underlying perceptual deficit in a child can materially reduce a behavioural disorder.

In considering delinquency, it is well to recognize that not all delinquents can be classified as behavioural disorders. Also, the term "delinquent" (8) encompasses a wide range of behaviour and may be defined by each profession within its own semantic system. Bovet (1) states that delinquency as seen by a psychiatrist and psychologist is but one of the many aspects of the elusive concept, "social maladjustment." He further notes that the child labelled delinquent suffers a secondary psychological reaction because of the attitude taken towards him by the "right" people: a boy with long hair is a boy with long hair and may have no tendency whatsoever to delinquency.

Studies on the primary prevention of delinquency have been difficult to assess because the definition of delinquency varies from community to community, and even the deviant behaviour is catalogued differently – a girl may be judged delinquent because of sexual relations but boys are seldom seen in juvenile court for this type of behaviour. Another factor impeding assessment has been the difficulty in matching controls: further projects quite often have been initiated in response to community crises.

Be that as it may, I would like to discuss briefly two projects which utilized social work principles. The first project, The Hyde Park Youth Project of Chicago (5) which bears the subtitle "A Co-ordinated Approach to the Prevention and Treatment of Youth Problems on a Neighborhood Basis" was under the direction of Charles Shireman of the Welfare Council of Chicago (a three-year programme, May 1955– May 1958). The demonstration area was a district two miles square within the environs of University of Chicago, having a population of 42,000, 66 per cent of which were white. At that particular time, this district was in the process of an urban renewal programme. The project group consisted of a core from the Welfare Council (director, supervisor, two case workers, dir. com. org. dir. research), partner agencies – for example, the Family Service Bureau, and youth bureaus of churches – and group workers drawn from the neighborhood club. Other community agencies, such as schools, the police department, city welfare, etc., were utilized. The aggressive child was accepted for referral on the premise that this child constituted a high risk for delinquent behaviour.

The 266 children showed the following characteristics: *age group*: 10–16; *racial distribution*: white 44 per cent; negro 52 percent; *sexual ratio*: 4 boys to 1 girl; *religion*: Protestant 51 per cent; Roman Catholic 25 per cent; unknown 19 per cent. The children showed an average of 2.3 behaviour problems with: 1 child out of 2 showing inability to accept controls, and 1 child out of 4 referred either for stealing or fighting. The main referral sources were the schools (50 per cent) and police (20 per cent). Of this latter group, no offence had been serious enough to warrant appearance in the juvenile court and yet the child was seen as having a tendency to delinquency. The academic profile showed 39 per cent of the children retarded by one year or more and 63 per cent of all the children with academic difficulties of which reading deficits were most common. Of the 231 families, in 45 per cent of cases both parents were found to be living in the home. Family disorganization, of a serious or a moderate degree, was found to be present in 52 per cent of all the families. Major areas of family conflict were marital difficulties, parent-child relationship, and individual personality adjustment.

The families were contacted by the project worker and the parents were not coerced into accepting help. The families were then either helped by the core project group or were given assistance by the participating agencies and groups. Fifty four per cent of the families were reported to have been reached and 17 per cent were considered to be unreachable. A typical family in the area included a mother from an impoverished family background, who had entered marriage to escape from intolerable home conditions, while the father had suffered from an inadequate father figure, was unable to hold a steady job, was passive, and had entered marriage to escape from his dominating mother. The marriage usually was dissolved shortly. Of the 110 children assessed for improvement it was found that 20 per cent made substantial gains and 45 per cent made some gain. The Hyde Park Project also included workers assigned to street gangs who had shown antisocial behaviour. Of the 326 members, 46 per cent (151) showed a reduction in deviant behaviour; 40 per cent (131) showed no change, but within this group there were 70 children who had not been previously known to have deviant behaviour. Thirteen per cent (42) were noted to be worse.

The second project, known as "Reaching the Hard-to-Reach" (9), the Huntington-Gifford project on hard-to-reach youth, was under the direction of Dr. Norman Roth, of Syracuse University School of Social Work. This study was over a three-year period (October 1957–October 1960) and was an effort to reach groups of adolescents by operating outside the bounds of legitimate community resources. This programme employed a professional social-work approach to determine whether these groups could be reached by a social worker and also to determine the characteristics of the groups. The subjects were identified on the basis of information available from neighborhood resources (for example, shopkeepers) and official agencies. In addition, instruments to evaluate individuals and groups were devised.

The intervention process consisted of a worker meeting with a small group twice a week using a car as a floating clubhouse. The worker set limits on acceptable group behaviour. The objective was to provide a real experience in which problems could be solved with the goal of helping an individual become aware of himself via the interaction between himself, the leader, and his peers. Four groups were selected for study; their over-all characteristics indicated that they came from a family background with weak or broken homes in lower and middle-class neighborhoods. The groups consisted of boys between 13 and 16 who had some delinquent experience (shoplifting, fighting, poor school work). They were motivated by a desire for fun, status, acceptance, and a prestige not available from the home; they used the group to achieve these ends and to fulfil their aggressive drives. The major findings of this study were that there were no well-organized gangs, but there were groups which consisted of clusters of individuals with a common bond; the individuals might each belong to other small clusters with different interests. There seemed to be no stereotyped individual; each boy was a distinct entity with his own behaviour patterns. Limits and controls were effective in producing positive responses. Progress was not smooth but occurred in spurts. It was also noted that behaviour modification occurred prior to any attitudinal change. Children who did not develop self-awareness were noted to be on the fringe and, when the study concluded, were the ones who got into trouble. A "Who am I?" and "Who are They?" rating scale was utilized to demonstrate changes.

In this paper I have attempted to give a brief view of the problem of primary prevention of behavioural disorders and delinquency. Some tentative conclusions may be made:

1. Deprivation (psychological) in early childhood can produce a behavioural disorder.

2. A behavioural disorder discovered on entering school may be prevented if the child enters a therapeutic day nursery and receives further assistance.

3. Recognition and treatment of a perceptually handicapped child may reduce a concomitant behavioural disorder.

4. Community leaders must face reality in dealing with behavioural disorders to provide the necessary environmental support to foster the total development of a child.

5. The delinquent and predelinquent child is amenable to change under certain conditions.

6. A community must become involved in delinquency prevention and control and must not deal with the problem by denial and avoidance.

REFERENCES

1. BOVET, B. *Psychiatric Aspects of Juvenile Delinquency*. Geneva: World Health Organisation, 1951. P. 9.
2. BOWLBY, J. *Maternal Care and Mental Health*. Geneva: World Health Organisation, 1951.
3. DE HIRSCH, KATRINA, *et al. Predicting Reading Failure*. New York: Harper and Brothers, 1966.
4. GOLDFARB, W. Emotional and intellectual consequences of psychological deprivation in infancy. In HOCH and ZUBIN (Eds.). *Psychopathology of Childhood*. New York: Grune and Stratton, 1955. Pp. 105–19.
5. *The Hyde Park Youth Project, May 1955–May 1958*. Welfare Council of Metropolitan Chicago.
6. JENKINS, R. L. Psychiatric syndromes in children and their relation to family background. *Amer. J. Orth.*, 1965, 36:450–57.

7. MALONE, C. A. Safety first: Comments on influence of external danger in the lives of children of disorganized families. *Amer. J. Orth.*, 1966, 37:3–12.
8. McLEOD, A. J. The juvenile delinquency committee. *Can. J. Corrections*, 6:43–9.
9. *Reaching the Hard to Reach.* Syracuse, N.Y.: The Huntington Family Center, Inc.
10. SHAW, DR. C. Personal Communication.

7   Some Methods of Primary Prevention

The General
Medical Practitioner/D. G. McKERRACHER, M.D.

What is the role of the non-psychiatric physician in the prevention of mental disorder? What can the medical practitioner do, in his office and in his hospital practice, to prevent some of the suffering of mental illness? Why is it most important to encourage the family physician in primary prevention?

What the non-psychiatric physician does to prevent mental disorder (or conversely to create iatrogenic illness) concerns us very much. Every day psychiatrists see patients whose anxiety is at least partly due to a lack of understanding by the family physician. I refer to the patient who is taking several dozen analgesic pills daily or to the woman who has just fractured some vertebrae in a withdrawal seizure after her sleeping pills had been discontinued. Public-health officers often grit their teeth with futility as they try to develop working arrangements with family physicians. Often hospital nurses agonize when they see patients cringe with anxiety as a result of statements from a thoughtless physician and, conversely, react with pleasure when the family doctor handles his patient with tact and kindness.

In discussing the role of the non-psychiatric physician in preventing the bad effects of mental disorder, I refer to all specialists as well as to the general practitioner. In the prevention of mental disorder the potential for good and evil of all doctors is great. Every day every physician sees patients with physical problems that have psychiatric components. Usually the psychiatric part is anxiety, depression, or confusion; it may or may not also have an organic accompaniment.

Anxiety goes with all somatic illness, however severe, from a simple respiratory infection to terminal carcinoma. Yet one third of the patients

seen by the general physician have no somatic underlay to their complaints – just pure anxiety or depression. The somatic complaints are
representative of anxiety ready to break through into the consciousness.
Consider the woman complaining of pounding of the heart. It is important that the family doctor understand that her real concern is that her
husband's business is in jeopardy, that she has six children, that she is
a Roman Catholic who has conflict over birth control, and that she is
disturbed by an over-critical parent.

The family physician must of course, make sure of his grounds when
he identifies a somatic complaint as a symbol of anxiety. It is important
that he not overlook the possibility of a thyroid condition or a cardiac
disorder. For this reason his physical investigation must be efficient, but
from a psychiatric standpoint the way in which he carries out this
investigation is most important. I am not implying that all patients react
in the same way to physical or laboratory examination; to some these
are supportive, whereas to others they are threatening. The point is that
the doctor must have in mind how the patient is likely to react when
under investigation. It is also important that he know how to get help
from the psychiatrist when he needs it. Sending a patient to a psychiatrist
can sometimes produce rather than prevent anxiety. The family physician
must establish rapport and trust before he can call in a consultant,
especially one so potentially anxiety producing as a psychiatrist.

Although anxiety is the most prevalent mental symptom, the non-
psychiatric physician must also know something about preventing depression. Most depressed patients come to their family doctors with somatic
complaints. I think of a 56-year-old man who had insomnia. He was
given a sleeping pill, but this was of no help. He then complained of loss
of energy and so received Dexadrine. He said he was weak and so
received vitamins. He then complained of loss of appetite and constipa-
tion and there followed a long drawnout study of the G.I. tract to rule
out carcinoma. Several weeks later and 35 pounds lighter, he was
referred to psychiatry. By this time he looked so cachectic that we subjected him to more physical examinations before electroconvulsive
therapy was applied to ease his suffering. Within the next two weeks he
gained 10 pounds and within three months 35 pounds. Had the family
doctor used more diagnostic skill in regard to depression he could have
prevented much of this misery. To me, this is primary prevention.

Now a word about prevention in the realm of senility. Have we something here to teach the family doctor? I think of an old man, living with
his daughter and grandchildren, who was becoming progressively more
senile. At first he was the object of great affection but as the spells of

confusion increased the family became disturbed. They referred him to the family physician who showed little interest. He became more and more preoccupied with thoughts of death, which he discussed with his grandchildren. One day, he mistook a neighbour's child for one of his own grandchildren and asked about her preparation for after-life. This led quickly to action and he was hustled off, permanently, to a mental hospital. In this situation the non-psychiatric physician could have done much for this family by preparing them to accept and deal with the increasing senility. Then the old man would not have so disturbed the neighbourhood that it became impossible for him ever to return there. Dr. Duncan McMillan of Nottingham often admits senile patients to mental hospitals for short periods of time, but before he does so, he prepares the family for the patient's quick return home.

The question becomes one of teaching the family doctor to deal with the prevention of mental disorder by teaching him the early signs of decompensation and how to deal with these. Many techniques of teaching have been tried; lectures, refresher courses, and Balint-type seminars. At the University Hospital in Saskatoon, we have found the best way to get response from family doctors is to let them handle those of their own patients who are in hospital suffering from anxiety, depression, or confusion. This is learning methods of prevention through consultation and supervision.

We started a programme with family doctors ten years ago. For the first seven years, we had one physician who admitted to two beds on the psychiatric ward. We looked over his shoulder as he dealt with early anxiety, depression, and senility. He learned much about attenuating developing disorder and this, for his patients, was good prevention. Some thought he did so well simply because of his own particular interest. The question was asked whether this could be repeated with other physicians. Many thought that most general practitioners would not want to treat their own psychiatric patients in a psychiatric ward, they thought the general practitioner preferred to be left alone to work with pills and scalpel. To find out, we set aside four beds. When the general practitioners referred patients, they were asked whether they wished to admit and treat these patients themselves. Of the first twenty we questioned, seventeen said they would like to treat their own patients with some help from psychiatrists, and all did. Of the next twenty, sixteen gave the same answer. As a result, we have permanently set aside four beds in the Department of Psychiatry to which general practitioners may treat their own patients. They come daily to see their patients, work with nursing-team leaders and with the medical students, and every week sit in a psychiatric conference. They retain responsibility for the patient, even though the psychiatrist is available to help when asked. These doctors are learning primary prevention.

Although this programme was fine for family physicians in a city where there was a psychiatric unit and where psychiatrists were close by, what could be done in the country? We found out four years ago when three country doctors said they wished to handle all the patients in their own 30-bed general hospital. They wanted us to help them organize this and to act as consultants. We worked out a programme to help these three doctors deal with anxiety, depression, and confusion in their practice. It was agreed that the general practitioners would look after all the psychiatric patients themselves, that a psychiatrist would be readily available for telephone consultations and would spend half a day with them every two weeks. This programme has been carried on for three years. It was set up as a research programme, so it is about to terminate, but the provincial government has arranged to provide psychiatric consultants to continue it on a permanent basis. These physicians now realize that psychiatry is a part of their general medical practice, and we consider that they are doing excellent primary prevention in a rural setting.

Is there anywhere else we can introduce preventive techniques to the practising physician? We believe that it is rather late to start with the doctor once he has entered practice. Like most psychiatrists, we think the best place to begin is with medical students, and that patients make the best teachers. After seven years of using medical students in looking after psychiatric patients we have found it wise to increase greatly their responsibilities. Now, each student spending a month in the Department of Psychiatry has major responsibility for from five to seven patients. He does the initial work-up, makes out a treatment plan, writes orders (under a complicated system of safeguards) and looks after emergencies. All this is done with a psychiatrist looking over his shoulder but from a reasonable distance. The students like this responsibility very much and the nurses have enthusiastically accepted the programme. The patients thrive under it and we believe that it is teaching the students primary prevention.

I would like to emphasize that primary prevention in psychiatry must become a major responsibility for the medical profession. All doctors can best learn the techniques of preventing anxiety and the ravages of depression and senility by themselves looking after most of their patients with psychiatric disorder. They should begin doing this as under-graduates, continue in a supervized situation as interns, and from then on through consultation contacts with psychiatric specialists. Thus they will become able to do a good deal of primary prevention as part of their daily work.

Public Education and
School Procedures / J. D. GRIFFIN, M.D.

It is the purpose of this presentation to review some of the attempts which have been made in recent years to protect and promote the mental health of children and adults through educational techniques. This is a difficult task, for presumably it would include the whole range of adult public mental-health education, college, high school, and elementary school procedures down to pre-kindergarten, nursery school, and day-nursery programmes. Obviously, all we can do here is to select some typical projects to help stimulate enquiry and discussion and hopefully to assist in evaluating the procedures which may be useful in the primary prevention of mental illness. The projects selected are not necessarily the best – nor do they represent all the types of projects which might be significant. They are merely the ones with which I am personally familiar and in some of which I have actually participated. Because of time I shall not deal here with the new emerging emphasis on sex education, or family life education as it is usually called in schools, although this undoubtedly has significance for mental hygiene. Nor shall I deal with college mental-hygiene programmes or programmes directed to the teachers' personal mental-health. These are topics which merit the emphasis of a separate consideration.

Public education, as we know it today, is a relatively late development in the western world. Total global impact has become not only possible but commonplace. However, three-hundred years ago public education was a pretty deliberate process concerned only with teaching knowledge and skills to the young. The purpose was clear, the methods simple and well defined, and the result not without its mental-health implications. The first education act ever passed in North America seems to have been legislation passed in the Commonwealth of Massachusetts in 1647. It was referred to popularly as "The Old Deluder, Satan Act" (1). The chief purpose of this Act seems to have been to teach children to read, so that when that old Deluder, Satan (or the free thinkers), tempted them with sinful ideas, all they had to do was to read the Bible, the only truly reliable book and, indeed, the only one generally available. This, it was believed, would give the child (or the adult, for that matter) all the answers, resolve all his doubts, and protect him from moral and social downfall. The mental health of such a child was almost bound to be pretty good because there was never reason for conflict or doubt. Everyone, especially the children, knew exactly what was right and wrong, what he could and could not do. The value systems were God-given, simple, sharp, and clear. Of course, there were occasional problems when contagious hysteria, hostility, and prejudice masquerading as heroic virtues combined to create and condemn a few witches. But these were promptly dealt with!

Compare our present situation. Values and moral and social codes are rapidly changing. Even as they change they are being ever more actively questioned and criticized. Certainly the old-style platitudes, taught to children in public and Sunday schools alike, are no longer regarded as useful or even correct. "Honesty is the best policy" is accepted only with the cynical and materialistic addition: "so long as it pays!"

In the light of uncertain values and changing moralities the role of a growing child in society is immeasurably more difficult for him to understand. His sense of security and identity, his awareness of limits, his expectations of others are all much less clear and less certain than they used to be. Instead of an adult society that is perfectly sure of both the desirable behaviour for children and the acceptable behaviour for grown-ups, he is gradually becoming aware of the fact that adults are even less sure of social and moral values and roles than he is. But this the adults will seldom admit. It is with this chaotic social system in mind that we must now address ourselves to the task of searching for ways in which the school can help build patterns of positive mental health in the personalities of our children and, hopefully, by the same token, help prevent psychiatric breakdown.

APPROACHES TO POSITIVE MENTAL HEALTH

In order to set the stage a little more for our discussion, it should be recognized that these two goals – attaining positive mental health and preventing mental breakdown – are by no means necessarily the same. Probably Jahoda's analysis of current approaches to positive mental health provides one of the best overviews of these goals (2). Very briefly, she categorizes the studies which have been and are being conducted in this field into six types:

1. *Attitude to self*: the degree of accurate self-perception possessed by a person.

2. *Self Actualization*: the degree to which he can utilize his potential.

3. *Synthesis*: the degree to which he is able to integrate his often ambivalent and conflicting psychic forces: the degree of personal integration, organization, and maturation.

4. *Autonomy*: the degree of social and personal independence he is able to achieve.

5. *Reality Perception*: the degree of accuracy with which he perceives external events, and phenomena.

6. *Environmental Mastery*: the degree of control he is able to exercise over external factors and events.

In reviewing these, one is reminded of some of the admonitions of the ancient Greek philosopher so often quoted by Dr. Hincks. He felt that good mental health was a matter of "knowing thyself, accepting thyself and being thyself." Tucker and LeRiche, after a very careful study of the same subject, arrived at practically the same conclusion (3). It is sometimes hard to avoid becoming cynical about these concepts and wondering if all we need to add is "to thine own self be true" and, with Kipling, "And – which is more – you'll be a Man, my son!"

But, seriously, can these concepts be taught to children as a concrete and integral part of the education process? Can they be included in the curriculum? Can we educate children truly to be autonomous, to have accurate perceptions of reality, to be masters of their environment? Perhaps. We can certainly keep these principles and goals in mind when we teach social studies, English literature, and the new maths. But a separate course in positive mental health? I doubt it.

Dr. Walter Barton is one psychiatrist who doubts the value of such a theoretical approach (4). He prefers the practical, objective, approach of the clinician. As one used to working with sick people he views health as that condition which prevails in a human being before he developed his sickness and after he has completely recovered from it. For him, good mental health is not a positive concept which is philo-sophically and scientifically separate and different from mental ill-health. The two conditions coincide. And mental health therefore is the absence of signs and symptoms of mental illness and psychiatric disorder. Such an approach seems to fit more easily the medical concepts of disease prevention and control.

As a physician he favours the idea of the physiologist, Walter Cannon, who developed the principle of homeostasis, meaning a stable equi-librium within the body. By extension he feels it could relate also to a state of equilibrium or balance between the internal and external environment. Thus good health is not something separate from disease but is related to preventive measures and successful treatment. "If you are not sick, you are well."

Such an approach opens the door to the possibility of intervention in a potential crisis or stress situation. It could be argued that this simpler and less theoretical approach still makes it possible for the teacher to think of prevention in terms of anticipating problems rather than merely spotting them after they have developed. And effective means of antici-patory intervention may well be one of the most practical techniques in primary prevention (5). Nevertheless, keeping both these approaches in mind let us review briefly the problem of prevention and the possibilities presented by the educative process.

SOME BASIC ASSUMPTIONS

It has been generally accepted for years, almost without serious question, that if we are ever to develop preventive techniques in the mental-health field it will be through work with children. Theoretically, if we only knew enough about the many genetic, constitutional, and environmental factors influencing personality development, and if these factors were subject to control, it would be possible to both prevent the onset of mental illness and promote the strengthening of positive mental health. But obviously such efforts would have to be instituted as early as pos-sible in the life of the individual – preferably at birth.

From the practical viewpoint of public-health planning, such a pro-gramme would have to be one applicable to large numbers of the population and would have to be under some sort of scientific and professional control. While there is evidence to show that sub-standard housing, crowded slums, poor or absent recreation facilities, inadequate parents or broken homes, poverty, even faulty or insufficient nourish-ment, all are potential factors in increasing the risk of mental break-down, it is the school which provides the mental hygienist with the most obvious practical setting in which to work. Here are gathered together nearly all the children of the community, in a controlled setting, five days a week for several hours a day. Their programme of activity is directed by professionals who, theoretically, are amenable to orientation, learning, collaboration, and supervision, and who operate within an administrative framework that is, again theoretically, favourable to the goals of mental health. In other words, the objectives of modern educa-tion almost always include references to the importance of helping children to develop a healthy personality, and frequently the concepts of positive mental health similar to those of Jahoda are spelled out.

Furthermore, most of the school systems in the larger Canadian urban areas now have a system of special educational and health services. These are directed variously to the child handicapped by retardation or physical disability, as well as to those with special educational problems, such as reading and speech disorders, and even to those with exceptional talent. Educational and clinical psychologists, social workers and teachers with training in mental health are being employed as fast as they become available. In the larger metropolitan areas psychiatric clinics are available, provided either by the school system itself (Toronto), the municipal health authority (Vancouver), or the provincial health department (Winnipeg). While all these services are primarily focussed on the child who has already been identified as one having a problem, they all stress the importance of early diagnosis, treatment, and prevention.

THE PRE-SCHOOL SETTING

Most Canadian schools now provide kindergarten classes for children at the age of five and, in some, pre-kindergarten or nursery school classes have been started. The value of the stimulus provided by such classes in developing social and language skills, motor co-ordination, and even in raising the IQ level has been demonstrated frequently (6). Their importance in correcting the effect of social and cultural deprivation is now being emphasized again. Sometimes the results are dramatic.

Two years ago Mrs. Barbara Frum, a volunteer working with the Canadian Mental Health Association, undertook to provide a weekly preschool experience for a group of 15 children from a downtown Toronto area (7). These three- and four-year-old children showed all the usual signs of lack of intellectual, cultural, and social stimulation. They were apathetic, non-verbal, incurious, disinterested, and dispirited little children. Usually they came from homes where both parents were working. Every Saturday morning Mrs. Frum, with two high-school girls as helpers, collected these children and conducted what was essentially a nursery-school type of programme. This consisted of visits to such institutions as a car wash, or a fire hall, a museum, or, on rainy days, a session of reading aloud, playing games, or perhaps using crayons and paper in a church basement. Perhaps the stimulation of all these activities was not as important as the presence of warmly responsive adult "mother figures." The result after seven months was an amazing growth of verbal, social, and emotional vitality in these children.

Of course this was not a scientifically designed or controlled study. But it is typical of what is being done on a larger scale in several school systems where pre-kindergarten classes have been started. In some, volunteers have been recruited simply to spend time with certain children as affectionate "Moms." The contrast with what happens when children such as these are neglected until grade one or two is obvious. By this time it seems that it may be too late to overcome the social and cultural lag. They become identified as "dull, disinterested, unable to concentrate, perhaps retarded."

Some interest has been shown in surveying preschool children with a view to determining their readiness for school. When this can be systematically carried out there are many advantages. It brings the mothers into contact early with both the school and health authorities, it facilitates the early detection of many potential physical and psychological problems which with suitable intervention and guidance may be prevented or quickly resolved.

Beaudet's account of a project of this kind undertaken by the health unit at Grand'Mère, P.Q. is an excellent example (8). His findings in the county of Laviolette showed a high incidence of psychological disorders affecting about half of all the children examined. He rightly points out the need for greater knowledge of mental hygiene on the part of the personnel of the health unit. Such knowledge also paves the way for early co-operative preventive work with the mental-health clinics and the school services.

Finally one should mention the efforts that have been made by many home and school associations as well as other community groups to organize courses in child rearing and management for parents of pre-school and school age children. Such parent-education courses are very difficult to evaluate in terms of effectiveness. At the best they serve to comfort and relax many parents who believe they have children with insoluble behaviour problems. They find that their children are not so different from others and the expression and verbalization of feelings of guilt and anxiety could have a therapeutic and hygienic effect. At the least, these courses provide a setting for a few parents, who have already developed an intellectual interest in child growth and development and a sophisticated approach to problems of child management to exchange views. One could believe, perhaps a little cynically, that among the vast army of worried parents this latter group needs help, guidance, and comfort most of all (9).

THE ELEMENTARY SCHOOL

The Elementary and Junior High Schools have been the setting for a number of projects aimed at primary prevention. Three different programmes will be described briefly here as typical of these.

1. *The Ojemann (Iowa) Project* (10)

Beginning in the early 1940s and continuing until the present, Professor Ojemann has been working extensively to design educational methods which are aimed specifically at the development of positive mental health in children. More precisely, his goal is to reduce emotional conflict in the classroom, and to increase mutually satisfying relationships among both children and teachers. His method is to teach children (and teachers) to appreciate the differences between overt (popular and superficial) interpretations of human behaviour and a more psychodynamic understanding. He constantly stresses the importance of understanding the "why" of behaviour rather than the more common practice of making judgments "about" behaviour. Thus he directs attention to human motivation, the multiple causation of behaviour, and the importance of establishing a range of values, rather than the more familiar "right" and "wrong," "good" and "bad" judgments. His programme is directed, of course, to teachers, who receive intensive training in mental-health concepts, to children, whom he involves in all grades from four to twelve, and to the curriculum itself, which he feels must be radically revised. He points out that, traditionally, the courses of study are laden with obsolete judgments about people: he was good, she was lazy, and so on. He feels that a much more meaningful and dynamic interpretation of human behaviour can be introduced by rewriting the curriculum especially for such subjects as English, social studies, home economics, and family life education. The method is based largely on discussion procedures during which the deeper and more dynamic meaning of human behaviour is explored.

He is currently preparing texts and manuals relating to his method which will be of great interest to mental hygienists everywhere. He also has been careful to establish his programme on a research basis so that constant evaluation with comparison to control groups is possible.

Results so far have provided convincing evidence that children exposed to a teaching and learning experience of this kind are more secure, more able to develop satisfying relations with others than are children who have not had this experience.

2. *The Woodlawn (Chicago) Project* (11)

A very different approach is that of Kellem and Schiff working in a mental-health clinic setting with children attending nine public and three separate schools in suburban Woodlawn. Challenged by the problem of primary prevention they first studied the prevalence of behaviour which might logically be symptomatic of early emotional or mental disorder among children in grade one. They found that the teachers, with a little coaching, could quite accurately spot those children showing such early signs of maladjustment as "shy" and "aloof," "over aggressive," "immature," "underachieving," and "over-active and restless." Checking the teachers' appraisals by means of psychiatric examinations they found close agreement. The process of assessing the children was repeated several times so that the teachers became very observant and skilled in this task. By careful followup they discovered that by the end of the first three months in school, 70 per cent of the children in grade one had some observable difficulty in behaviour. A five-point adjustment rating scale ranging from "satis-factory" to "very disturbed" was established. Thirty-six per cent were rated as having mild problems, 19 per cent as moderately severe, and 14 per cent as quite disturbed. Close psychiatric study indicated that at least half of the last group (or 7 per cent of the total) were really seriously disturbed children.

With these studies as a background, Kellem and Schiff then instituted a three-part programme. The first comprised a weekly session with each class of children led by the psychiatrist. These sessions were very informal and dealt with the ordinary problems and feelings which small children experience in school. They were called "counselling sessions" and were quite permissive. The children were encouraged to talk about their feelings. Suggestions were freely advanced as to how they might cope with these feelings in effective and successful ways. The second part of the programme consisted of a weekly counselling session with the teachers by the psychiatrist individually or, more usually, in small groups. The third part was a periodic discussion group with the parents of the children led by the psychiatrist.

The programme was established on a research basis with a control group and repeated assessments of the children's behaviour and person-ality by both teachers and psychiatrists. The results at the end of the first year revealed that the experimental group of children had an 8.2 per cent rise in satisfactory adjustment while the control group showed a 0.8 per cent fall. These results were felt to be quite encouraging, especially in view of the increasing divergence of effect between the experimental group and the control.

The project is a very neat example of many other programmes which are currently underway, some of them in Canada. They involve a very close working relationship between a mental-health clinic team and the school. Quite characteristically the core of such projects is the "consultation" which takes place in connection with a child showing signs of significant emotional disorder. This consultation involves the teacher, the principal, the school nurse, the guidance teacher, the school psychologist, and the clinic team. The information from and interpretations made by each of these is pooled, with the primary purpose of assisting and supporting the classroom teacher who is encouraged to handle the problem himself if possible. Variations on this theme are encountered frequently. Sometimes a home visit is indicated or perhaps the parent is invited to "sit in" at the consultation. Sometimes the family doctor comes and sometimes representatives of community social agencies who have an interest in the child. In one semi-rural area a psychiatrically oriented general practitioner has been holding regular consultations (counselling) sessions with teachers in the junior high school with apparently good results (12).

There is much to commend this relatively simple but very revealing approach. The teacher quickly learns that he is not alone in his problem and that others know something about the family or the child and are ready to help. All benefit by developing an appreciation of the many resources available in the school and the community. About the only complaint with these "consultations" is the time they take. Frequently more than an hour is used up in discussing one case and this apparently causes some difficulty in scheduling the timetables. It seems to me, however, that it is precisely this sort of administrative question which must be overcome if we are to implement sound mental hygiene programmes in the school.

3. *The Toronto Human Relations Classes*

Impressed by the technique of informal group discussions among high-school students, demonstrated by Dr. Alice Keliner of Columbia Teachers College in 1937, Line, Griffin, and, later, Seeley and Mallinson developed and assessed the procedure commonly called "Human Relations Classes" in various schools of the Toronto area and particularly in Forest Hill Village (13, 14). Originally the technique relied on the stimulus provided by a short excerpt from a popular movie involving children (the film, *Captains Courageous,* furnished several such episodes) in order to start the discussion rolling. The technique was very similar to that later developed by Ojemann in his classes. The teacher acting as discussion leader encouraged the children to think about the causality of behaviour and the underlying motives at play, and the devices and behaviour used to obtain the desired goals and so on. Later, short narratives related informally by the teacher were substituted for the film excerpts, and later still the class chose their own topic – whatever was of urgent interest and importance to them at that particular time. As the discussion became group-directed, the teacher diminished in importance as a leader. He became increasingly a resource person and often just an observer.

The procedure was regarded with some suspicion by school officials and many teachers because the objectives seemed to be unclear. There was no lesson plan and, above all, there was no way to evaluate the children to see if they had learned anything! But of course it was precisely these attributes of the experience that made it so valuable. The children learned to listen to one another, to think for themselves, to evaluate critically the judgments of others, and finally to reach decisions which they could recognize as tentative but, more importantly, as their own and to which they could allow themselves to be committed. These special classes were held weekly for a regular classroom period in grades 6 to 12. Not all teachers found it easy to learn to be so permissive and some seemed to become overtly anxious and disturbed at what they felt to be a lack of control over a potentially chaotic situation. However, those teachers who had sufficient experience and training to give them a sense of security in the classroom and an appreciation of the objectives of the exercise could, with training, practice, and the support of the consultant, develop excellent skills in the technique.

Psychiatrists generally are worried lest such permissive procedures become essentially group-therapy sessions in which acute anxieties in some children may arise which the teachers will not know how to handle. Actually in the experience in the Toronto area such crises seemed never to arise. Perhaps the discussion never became sufficiently personal or never related to deeply repressed material. However, the similarity to "group dynamic sessions" cannot be denied.

In evaluating the results one could not fail to be impressed by the enthusiasm expressed by the children themselves for these classes. In addition Mallinson showed conclusively, by means of both objective tests and qualitative judgments of the teachers (not to mention the results of the final exams!), that the children in these classes gained significantly on all fronts related to social, emotional, and intellectual adjustment as compared with the control group.

SOME ROAD BLOCKS

While the schools would thus seem to be the obvious area for developing programmes of primary prevention, it should be admitted that they are by no means ideal. Many school systems, for instance, still have a heavy emphasis on competition, regimentation, grading examinations, and closely supervized and rigidly adhered to courses of study. The impact of this kind of school climate has an adverse effect on the mental health of many children. In other words it must be admitted that although the school setting seems to be a natural one for scientific efforts aimed at the primary prevention of mental illness, this same school setting often actually contributes to children's psychiatric problems (15).

Generally speaking, the school administration places a major emphasis on achievement as represented by examination and test results. In addition to providing a highly competitive setting in which the children are expected to learn, to achieve, and even to excel, the system tends to be relatively inflexible in terms of the size of class, the grade system, the timetable, and the curriculum. The emphasis seems to be directed toward developing a complacent if not harmonious relationship between everyone concerned: pupils with teachers, pupils with pupils, and teachers with teachers. Rather than having a positive interest in prevention, the school system seems to be more interested in providing an increasing number of special services for groups of handicapped and exceptional children.

In addition, there seems to be a reluctance in many teachers and especially in some of the school officials to accept a close working collaboration with other professionals on a truly interdisciplinary basis. These attitudes are not a reflection on the personalities of teachers and educational leaders. It reflects in part the political sensitivity of elected school boards and trustees. They honestly feel they cannot advance beyond what they discern to be the opinion and attitude of the majority of the electorate – including, but not necessarily limited to, the parents. In part too it reflects the very natural tendency of the administrative and supervisory group to protect the status quo of the system, including their own careers and those of the teachers (Frieser, 16).

The reaction which the students themselves have to the school system and its teachers is sometimes revealing. While most of the children are content to carry on without complaint or overt rebellion, there is an increasing group of young people, particularly in high schools, who are not loath to show their discontent. Frequently they become dropouts and as such they sometimes seem to carry a certain social stigma. But for them the schools seem to be represented by such scathing terms as "scab labs of conformity." It is not sufficient to dismiss this minority group as comprising only the misfits, educational ne'er-do-wells and trouble makers. The schools as well as society in general have failed somehow to find how to help these youngsters grow into mature and effective people.

Finally the classroom teachers, reflecting the feelings and interpreting the attitudes of the school authorities, necessarily are concerned, not so much with the children they teach, as with the completion of tasks, discipline and control. Most teachers, however, will express a deep interest in knowing more about children and about the dynamics of behaviour. They feel that they lack skill in this field and that far too little time has been spent on mental health and human relations in their basic training. Like the school system itself, the training of teachers has tended to become quite inflexible and subject-oriented rather than child-oriented.

As these difficulties are more clearly identified and understood they may begin to disappear. The gradual acceptance of longer training courses for teachers and the increasing demand for teachers who are university graduates should help.

PUBLIC EDUCATION AND PREVENTION

Quite apart from the efforts to introduce preventive techniques into the school system, educational efforts directed to the public at large have been attempted in various ways for many years without conclusive results. The mass media of all kinds have been and are still being employed for this purpose. Mass education about the nature of mental illness, its causes, its treatment, and the mental-health facilities available in the community undoubtedly have improved public knowledge to some extent. Efforts to educate the public about mental hygiene and preventive procedures are of course harder to evaluate. Lectures, pamphlets, books, press stories, editorials, and even comic strips, radio, television, and movies have all been used extensively.

Improvement in the general public's knowledge of mental illness and health can be measured to some extent by repeated questionnaires, surveys, Gallup polls, and studies on changing practices (17). The gain in public knowledge is offset by the very persistent stigma: an emotional reaction which still seems to characterize the field of mental illness and even the professional people working in it. Furthermore I know of no evidence that public awareness or understanding of mental illness ever really prevented such illness from developing.

We can state with some confidence at this time, however, that if highly motivated groups such as teachers, public-health nurses, clergy, and physicians are helped to develop an understanding of children and parents and families in a mental-health context, at least the stage would be set for the next step: a move into secondary and perhaps even primary prevention.

REFERENCES

1. SINCLAIR, D. Personal Communication, January 1967.
2. JAHODA, M. *Current Concepts of Positive Mental Health* Mon. Series No. 1. Joint Commission on Mental Illness and Health, New York: Basic Books, Inc., 1958.
3. TUCKER, D. K. and W. H. LeRICHE. Mental health: the search for a definition. *Can. med. assoc. J.*, 1964, 90:1160–66.
4. BARTON, W. Viewpoint of a clinician, *Ibid.*, 2, chap. VII.
5. CAPLAN, G. Opportunities for school psychologists in primary prevention of mental disorders in children. *Ment. Hyg.*, 1963, 47:525.
6. BLATZ, W. E. *Human Security: Some Reflections.* Toronto: University of Toronto Press, 1966.
7. FRUM, B. The deprived child. Unpublished report presented to the Annual Conference, Ontario Division, Canadian Mental Health Assoc., 1965.
8. BEAUDET, A. L'aspect psycho-social dans l'examen Préscolaire. *Can. J. pub. Hlth*, 1966, 57:519.
9. SEELEY, J. R. *et al.* Crestwood Heights, Toronto: University of Toronto Press, 1956.
10. OJEMANN, R. H. Basic approaches to mental health: the human relations program at the state university of Iowa. *Pers. guid. J.*, 1958, 36:198.
11. KELLEM, S. G. and SCHIFF, S. K., "A Community-Wide Mental Health Program of Prevention and Early Treatment in First Grade" APA Psych. Rep./21 (Poverty and Mental Health) 1967.
12. COLLYER, J. A. Seminars for senior public school teachers. Unpublished report to the Canadian Medical Association Committee on Mental Health, 1966.
13. GRIFFIN, J. D. and J. R. SEELEY. Education for mental health: an experiment. *J. Can. Ed.*, 1952.
14. MALLINSON, T. J. An experimental investigation of group-directed discussion in the classroom. Unpublished PhD. thesis, Dept. of Psycholoy, University of Toronto, 1954.
15. STOGDILL, C. G. School achievement, learning difficulties and mental health. Supplement No. 48, CMH, Sept.–Oct. 1965.
16. FREISER, L. H. The system that strangles learning. *Globe and Mail*, Toronto, Mar. 29, 1967.
17. SILVERMAN, B. Changes in practices study. Unpublished report of the Public Education Committee to the National Scientific Planning Council of the Canadian Mental Health Association, 1954.

Crisis Theory and
Preventive Intervention/VICTOR SZYRYNSKI, M.D.

With the rapid development of community psychiatry all workers in the field became acutely aware of the considerable shortage of professional resources to undertake the task of the expanding programmes of mental health protection. Consequently, their attention has been focussed on obtaining maximal effects through promoting better efficiency and greater economy of professional efforts. The first problem has been taken care of by developing new training programmes in community psychiatry for all professional divisions and also by further emphasizing the importance of in-service training at different levels of competence. The problem of economy stimulated the development of new concepts and new techniques to obtain the best results from any professional intervention. It has been noticed that mental health assistance provided promptly at the critical periods of life of an individual, or of a social group, makes possible better and more far-reaching results with a relatively minimal outlay of professional time and effort. It was also noticed that focussing co-operation of many elements of the mental health personnel at such moments would carry still further the principle of economy.

THE MAIN CHARACTERISTICS OF CRISIS SITUATION

The crisis theory in community psychiatry emphasizes the importance of situations of crisis during the normal development of an individual and in the unexpected stressful experiences in his life. The concept of emotional stress is not new in psychiatry and was usually understood as a situation when defence mechanisms in a personality are mobilized to cope with the stressful emergency. The concept of crisis emphasizes that not only mobilization but also very important reorganization of adjustive mechanisms takes place. This reorganization may eventually result in an elevation or abasement of the mental health level in the personality. An individual would emerge from a crisis situation either more mature and better able to cope with future stressful experiences or more regressed with more disorganized personality which under further stress may reach the level of a mental illness. Already some years ago, Leo Alexander (1) recommended classification of defence mechanisms in terms of their relative value for maintaining the mental health of the personality. It is also possible to think about ego-strength of an individual in terms of the calibre of defences which he uses in maintaining homeostasis in his emotional adjustment to reality.

It has also been observed that during a crisis situation there exists markedly enhanced susceptibility to therapeutic intervention. The immediate presence and efficiency of such assistance very often determines the outcome of crisis; whether it will result in a higher level of adjustment or lead towards greater disintegration. It is claimed that assisting an individual to face reality leads to his mobilizing defences of a higher level. Instead of denying a problem, a patient is helped to face it in a more realistic manner and "to do something about it." Even with minor assistance it is possible to promote better decision-making abilities in an individual. We may possibly remark here that "paradoxical intention" (4) in the psychotherapeutic approach may probably be considered a technique which assists in constructive decision-making by exaggeratedly over-emphasizing the reality principle.

CRISIS SITUATIONS IN HUMAN LIFE

Caplan classifies crisis situations as "developmental" and "accidental" (2). Throughout his life every individual is forced to change his environment and to face new life situations which require reorganization of his mechanisms of adjustment. A small child enters kindergarten, then school, possibly later switches to a boarding school, goes to his first summer camp, then college, gets engaged, marries, has his first child, accepts his first job, may eventually change it, and assumes gradually more and more complex responsibilities. The accidental crises may include illness, operations, hospitalizations, death of a family member, loss of work, financial collapse, separation from significant individuals, and various other failures (or even some of the unexpected successes in connection with which Sigmund Freud described his "success neurosis"). Every psychiatrist remembers that even achieving most coveted promotions may lead to an acute depressive reaction.

A crisis situation may affect a single individual, the general population (as in mass disasters) or some circumscribed sub-populations exposed to special risks or additional stress, like students entering college, volunteers joining the Peace Corps, young people entering religious orders, military recruits, families of servicemen transferred overseas, unwed mothers entering sheltered institutions, etc. In all such circumstances an individual undergoes a reorganization as we have mentioned above. He may emerge from the crisis with better mental-health equipment or with a lowered stability and integration; because of this greater susceptibility to preventive intervention during a crisis the therapist can do much to determine the outcome of such a new experience.

The special-risk population groups may be subdivided either geographically or functionally (3). The examples of the latter have been discussed above. Under some circumstances a whole nation may present the situation of social disintegration. This usually results in marked increase in antisocial behaviour with raising prevalence of emotional and mental disorders. The collective efforts of such communities become less efficient while suspiciousness, hostility, and hatred begin to permeate their social climate.

MEANING AND EXAMPLES OF PREVENTIVE INTERVENTION

As mentioned above, individuals or social groups going through a crisis situation are particularly susceptible to preventive intervention. All efforts of assistance, if properly displayed, become economical and efficient. This assistance is classified as preventive psychiatry on the assumption that it prevents further disintegration of an individual and provides him, at resolution of the crisis, with a higher level of defensive organization. In addition to that, such intervention, even in cases where a particular individual goes through crisis, is usually aimed at a large number of "significant" people: family, foster homes, the college, etc. Such an intervention, therefore, becomes a social therapeutic action with far-reaching preventive qualities. From our personal studies I may quote an example of London children evacuated during the war to other localities in the country; taken away from their parents, their school, and their usual environment they certainly underwent a serious crisis situation. In studying their reactions to the new surroundings, it was interesting to note how much value they ascribed to assistance rendered by the first individuals who approached them in a friendly way in their new community. Such individuals were accepted unusually readily as models for identification, and strong dependence and attachment would rapidly develop. Undoubtedly one may find similar impressions in memories of immigrants settling in a new country. Such a reaction is probably well known to churches who send missions to ports of entry to meet the newcomers. In our programme of rehabilitation of unmarried mothers, we have found a rather similar reaction in those teenage girls who, during their stay in an institution, were exposed to a very active programme of therapeutic assistance consisting of bi-weekly conferences with a social worker, weekly discussions with a clergyman, and bi-monthly group psychotherapeutic contact with a psychiatrist. The latter would consist of reviewing their work with the social worker and discussing the questions submitted at the end of such sessions and presented to a psychiatrist. Most of such questions were concerned with the attitude of the girls when they would return to their families, their schools, and their communities, with their feelings about the pregnancy and disposition of their child, and with their attitudes towards their boyfriends and men in general, and also their relationship with parents. The emotional growth of the girls in response to the programme was rather astonishing and many of them, on leaving the institution, commented quite spontaneously that the programme was one of the most valuable experiences they had in their life. Undoubtedly, this experience had important preventive value for the future adjustment of those adolescents.

Understanding the nature of crisis intervention may also explain some interesting results of dynamic psychotherapy in cases when one or two interviews succeed in complete removal of symptoms and development of a much more mature pattern of adjustment. The two following cases may illustrate this point.

Case I: a 12-year-old girl has been brought to the psychiatrist with complaints of acute anxiety reaction marked by her inability to stay alone in her room, fear of going to school and general feeling of vague apprehension with fear of death. During the interview, this very bright girl related her experience of being pulled with another girl by a group of boys to a forest where the girls were subjected to sexual molesting. The whole situation was carefully discussed with the child and much sexual enlightment was provided during the interview which was generally maintained on the ego-supporting level. The patient was seen again in a week's time and both she and her mother reported complete disappearance of all the symptoms. A follow-up, two months later, confirmed total freedom from symptoms and very good adjustment to all areas of the child's life.

Case II: A girl of 14 was brought by a social worker to the psychiatric clinic with the following history: when she was thirteen and a half, she developed a strong attachment to a young man of 18; she went out steadily with him for a couple of months and then she became pregnant. They eloped and got married. A juvenile court interfered: the girl was placed in a protective institution and the boy sent to jail. The marriage was ruled invalid and a few weeks later the girl aborted. The court decided termination of parental rights and the girl was placed in a foster home 300 miles away from her original locality under the care of a childless couple of intelligent and very dedicated farmers who took a keen interest in her. During the second week after placement, the first psychiatric consultation was secured. When first seen the girl was rather withdrawn, defensive, and somewhat negativistic, with marked hostility. Psychotherapeutic approach was set in the ego-supportive way and her general reaction to the new home, new school, and community was discussed. Information from the social worker indicated an unusually poor family background. The child's original family was known to the whole community for their criminal exploits and their cohesive but strongly antisocial attitude.

The foster mother also had regular sessions with the psychiatrist and easy access to the social worker. It has been reported during the first few months of treatment that although the girl's outward behaviour was marked by conformity and rather constructive co-operation, she still held bitter resentment towards the court's order which separated her from her closely knit family. After about three months, the girl, who never dated boys in the new locality and had the most correct attitude towards her school friends, failed to return home; the foster parents received a call from her at about 4.00 o'clock A.M. from one of the local hotels. She informed them where she was and asked what she had to do next. The answer was very simple, "just come home as soon as you can." The foster father drove to the place and brought the child back home. After that episode, which on the psychiatrist's advice was rather disregarded, the child became much more affectionate towards the foster parents and during one of the psychiatric visits, she burst into tears, showing marked emotional upset. When asked for the reason she confessed that it was the eve of Mothers' Day and she had decided not to send a card to her real mother but to her foster mother whom she had finally selected and accepted in place of her own. Further adjustment to the family was entirely uneventful and the girl was eventually adopted by her foster parents.

It appears that crisis intervention should seriously be considered as the approach of choice in many cases of delinquency and criminal maladjustment. Among other conditions, school phobia has also been studied from that angle (7).

TECHNIQUE OF CRISIS INTERVENTION

Crisis intervention is a social act. It consists of a sympathetic, friendly contact with a person or a group experiencing crisis situation. Immediacy is one of its basic characteristics. Assistance should take place during the crisis situation and not long after. This principle has an important bearing on organizing helping facilities in the community. Another important feature is that in many cases initiative stays with the helper who is not waiting until the patient asks for assistance. In the case of communities suffering from collective disasters, help is promptly organized for the people. In individual cases, for example for a family who has lost its father in an accident, help is promptly available for the remaining family members. These two factors set crisis management distinctly apart from our customary psychotherapeutic habits. Crisis intervention is reality-oriented, it attempts to help an individual or a group to adjust to the current reality. It has been found that frequency is another feature of crisis intervention. The helping individual seeks frequent contacts with the person under stress. Assistance of pharmacological agents is applied sparingly; the drugs should not blur perception of reality. It is also important to allow an individual in crisis to go through appropriate emotional reactions of grief, mourning, etc. The "high-level" adjustment mechanisms such as concentration and identification are encouraged, while the negative escapes such as denial, projection, blaming others, and the like are counteracted as far as possible. The patient's environment is mobilized to participate in helping intervention: the family, the neighbours, the community agencies, the church, working companions, employers, etc. Necessary changes of life patterns are discussed with the patient. His cultural traditions as far as they may be of assistance in coping with the crisis are attentively considered.

WHO PROVIDES CRISIS INTERVENTION?

The philosophy of preventive psychiatry is community oriented. The notion of helpful intervention in crisis situations should be known to a great number of people, including psychiatrists, general physicians, members of the other professions concerned with mental health, the social workers, psychologists, clergymen, nurses, personnel managers, rehabilitation officers, judges, policemen, etc. Since psychiatrists have the advanced professional sophistication in the field of mental health, their efforts should be multiplied through close co-operation with the other individuals interested in assisting their fellow beings. When one thinks about developing a programme for prompt and efficient crisis intervention, the above-mentioned immediacy and urgency calls for easy availability of a helping agent. This means that the individual private psychiatric office is probably the least useful of the helping agents. We are turning, however, to general practitioners, to the emergency departments of the hospitals, to various social agencies in the community and – as far as psychiatric practice goes – to the large flexibly organized teams such as well-developed mental health clinics, psychiatric units in larger general hospitals, the community psychiatric hospitals, or the large provincial institutions. In organizing crisis intervention programmes, the main role of the psychiatrist would consist of providing initiative, assisting with organization, participating in the in-service (on the job) training of the wide range of personnel necessary and providing the very special type of services which are known as mental-health consultations. He would participate in different orientation and training programmes in the field of mental health, for example, for teachers, clergymen, police officers, etc. He would also take part in various community programmes oriented towards special risk subpopulations such as the unwed mother and immigrants, acting in such cases either as a direct participant in the programmes or as consultant.

The role of a general hospital in the organization of primary prevention has been often critically evaluated. "Whether a hospital unit is the appropriate centre for organizing and administering a community-wide mental health programme is a question which will require considerable thought. It is highly problematic whether hospitals, with their usual treatment-oriented programmes, possess either the resources or willingness to undertake programmes of primary prevention" (5). It appears that a fundamental change in its philosophy is indispensable. So far, hospitals have been functioning mostly on a defensive type of policy: being simply available whenever the patients turned to them for assistance. In the field of primary prevention the opposite orientation is necessary, based on the aggressive philosophy of moving actively into the community to organize or assist with programmes and services aiming at creation of a social climate which, as we believe, may prevent to a different degree the occurrence or severity of psychiatric disorders (6).

REFERENCES

1. ALEXANDER, E. *Treatment of Mental Disorders.* Philadelphia: Saunders, 1953.
2. CAPLAN, GERALD. *Principles of Preventive Psychiatry.* New York: Basic Books Inc., 1964. Pp. 34–35.
3. ———— A conceptual framework for preventive psychiatry. Mimeographed text. November 1965. Pp. 5, 13–14.
4. FRANKL, V. E. Paradoxical intention: a logotherapeutic technique. *Amer. J. Psychother.,* 1960, 14:520–35.
5. SCHULBERG, HUBERT C. Psychiatric units in general hospitals: boon or bane? Harvard School of Public Health, *Working Papers in Community Mental Health.* Spring 1963. P. 52.
6. SZYRYNSKI, V. The role of the general hospital in the community mental health program. In *Proceedings of the 33rd Annual Convention of the Catholic Hospital Conference of Ontario.* October 1966. P. 62.
7. WALDFOGEL, S., E. TESSMAN, and P. B. HAHN. A program for early intervention in school phobia. *Amer. J. Orthopsych.,* 1959, 29.